PRAISE FOR *MANAGING ORGANIZATIONAL CHANGE*

"Having a great strategy is only one element to gaining a competitive advantage; understanding how to manage the resulting change into your company is equally important. Every organization is different; what works for one will not work for another and it is often difficult to understand why and what should be done about it. The truly practical tools in this book will help experienced leaders looking for ideas to jump-start their change initiatives and those starting to build change capability for the first time. In the same way that other landmark books have turned out to be a timeless resource for managers, this book will become the guide for leaders to assess and build change capability for their organizations."

Caroline Perkins, Co-founder and President, Change Management Institute

"They say a picture paints a thousand words. Well this book has both. It is professional, sophisticated yet practical and easy to follow and understand. Change is about action. Not careless, reckless, thoughtless action but coordinated, well-orchestrated well-led plans. This book will help any leader or aspiring leader become a successful change agent.

Charles Darwin said… 'It is not the strongest of the species that survives, nor the most intelligent that survives. It is the one that is the most adaptable to change.' The same can be said about businesses or teams. Helen's book will help ensure you and your team SURVIVE!"

Pat Meyer, CEO, ICNet International

"This book is easy to read, presenting clear practical application grounded on sound theoretical perspectives. It is thought provoking and fully engages the reader whether novice or expert. It is equally well placed to support practical implementation or academic study."

Dr Alan R Dowler PhD BSc MBPsS, Senior Lecturer, Cardiff School of Social Sciences, Cardiff University

"This book is an essential guide to navigating the complex and challenging subject of organizational change. *Managing Organizational Change* is a no nonsense approach that challenges leaders to think through what it takes to change their business; to anticipate and drive beyond the lip service to change that change managers often encounter. It provides a clear and easy to follow framework, richly illustrated by case studies and examples that guides you through the organizational change process."

Ira Blake, author of Project Managing Change, and co-lead of the Change Management Institute UK

"Managing change is the Holy Grail for every organization. The path to successfully managing the benefits is all too often skewed by the people factor. Helen Campbell simplifies the complexity of managing change. Based on her years of experience she provides a practical and easy to apply approach and set of tools for tackling organizational change, including its traps of which the most diverse and difficult is the issue of managing the people involved or affected by change, all the while keeping an eye on a successful and profitable project outcome, moving the organisation forward."

Dr Janet V Cole, PhD, Principal Lecturer, Field Leader for Computing Studies, Kingston University

"This book is a 'must read' for anyone seeking to avoid the common pitfalls that cause so many organizational changes to fail, as it brings much needed clarity and structure to this subject."

Simon Ewin, Business Director, Chartered IT Professional, Telecommunications company

"An excellent read! A simple and powerful collection of practical and pragmatic frameworks that will help managers and leaders successfully implement change."

Suzanne Murray-Prior, Director, Change Management, Large consulting firm

"This is a really top-notch read. It is great that it starts by making the proposition that the business of change management needs to make a change itself – as the history of unsuccessful change programs is not a pretty one. The book is also very effective in developing a case and a roadmap for change that will resonate at the C-level because it makes the compelling connection between effective change and the return to the company's shareholders."

Paul Kell, Chairman, KickStart Thailand

"Helen's book is one of those rare times that a successful practitioner finds time to share their tips and techniques on how to manage organisational change well. It answers all those nagging doubts – that anyone has who has either initiated or been on the receiving end of change – as to 'whether there is a better way?'. It does so clearly, honestly and with that hard-to-find blend of pragmatism and theoretical strength."

Amanda Morgan, General Manager, Financial Services, ASX 100 company

Managing
Organizational
Change

Managing Organizational Change

A practical toolkit for leaders

HELEN CAMPBELL

KoganPage

LONDON PHILADELPHIA NEW DELHI

First published in Great Britain and the United States in 2014 by Kogan Page Limited

2nd Floor, 45 Gee Street
London EC1V 3RS
United Kingdom
www.koganpage.com

1518 Walnut Street, Suite 1100
Philadelphia PA 19102
USA

4737/23 Ansari Road
Daryaganj
New Delhi 110002
India

© Helen Campbell, 2014

Cycle of Change is the Trade Mark of Catalyst Business Solutions Pty Ltd.

The right of Helen Campbell to be identified as the author of this work has been asserted by her in accordance with the Copyright, Designs and Patents Act 1988.

ISBN   978 0 7494 7083 8
E-ISBN 978 0 7494 7084 5

British Library Cataloguing-in-Publication Data

A CIP record for this book is available from the British Library.

Library of Congress Cataloging-in-Publication Data

Campbell, Helen.
  Managing organizational change / Helen Campbell. – 1st Edition.
    pages cm
    ISBN 978-0-7494-7083-8 (pbk.) – ISBN 978-0-7494-7084-5 (ebk.)   1. Organizational change.
2. Leadership.   I. Title.
  HD58.8.C32156 2014
  658.4'06–dc23
                                                              2013049652

Typeset by Graphicraft Limited, Hong Kong
Print production managed by Jellyfish
Printed and bound by CPI Group (UK) Ltd, Croydon, CR0 4YY

Contents

Online resources to accompany this book are available from
www.koganpage.com/managingoc

Introduction

Dear Reader

It is likely that you're reading this because you have a desire or a need to improve the way your organization changes. Perhaps you have decided you are ready to build a change-ready organization. Obviously the first step is to read the book. When you've done that you'll have a range of good ideas which could bring real value to you, your colleagues, customers and investors. Wouldn't it be a shame if none of these improvements ever materialized and none of the potential value was created? Don't look on this just as a book for you to read – look on it as the start of a change initiative for you and your organization to improve the results you achieve from organizational change.

What you are about to read covers all types of change in a wide variety of organizations and sectors. It will provide insights into the whole change cycle. Plenty is written about the component parts of change: strategy, leadership, management, change, project and benefits management but changing your organization successfully requires you to take a view across these functions. The information in this book will enable you to identify and improve the parts of your organization that are helping the change and those that are holding you back. It provides the glue that binds all these traditional functions together to bring you the potential for more reliable investments and greater success.

Get interactive. Read the book with a pencil in your hand or your keyboard open on your e-reader. Mark the phrases that grab you, do the assessments, think about the results and actively consider each of the common traps and ideas for improvement. Use the template in Appendix 12 to keep a note of your organization's strengths and weaknesses so you can plan what to do about them.

Be honest. At various points in the book you will have the opportunity to assess current performance. Humans have a self-serving bias which means that we consistently think we are better than we are. Try to be as objective as possible and consider asking others for their perspective.

Every change and every organization is different. As you read the information in this book decide what your biggest weaknesses are and the relative impact and priority of each of them in the context of your change and your organization. When deciding which improvements to make you'll need a realistic understanding of the constraints you'll be working with.

Use the information in this book to:

- **Learn from others** so you don't waste time and effort reinventing the wheel.
- **Educate your organization** by outlining the real scope of organizational change.
- **Assess your performance** so you know what you do well and where your biggest gaps are.
- **Manage risks** by identifying the strategic, reputational, financial and operational risks associated with the way your organization manages change.
- **Celebrate and embed success** by identifying the norms, people, processes and systems that are currently helping change.
- **Inform decision makers** by identifying specific improvements with clear benefits.
- **Develop integrated frameworks and methodologies** that encompass the full range of activities required to make change successful.

Scoot around. If you are in a hurry go straight to the chapters that affect or interest you most. Chapter 1 provides some evidence of the common signs of poorly managed change. Chapter 2 outlines the Cycle of Change model and the component parts of organizational change. Chapter 3 provides insights into the four things your organization must *have* if it wants to change. Chapter 4 offers valuable information about the six things that need to be *done* well if change is going to be successful. Chapters 3 and 4 contain 100 traps that organizations commonly fall into that undermine their attempts at change. They also outline 100 ideas that can be adopted straight away; most of them without having to ask permission or hire consultants! Finally, Chapter 5 helps you bring it all together and build a robust plan of action. In the appendices you'll find some useful templates to help you assess and plan each component for your organization.

I'd love to hear what you think, so please contact me at **helen@catalyst-solutions.com.au** or check out the websites **www.cycleofchangemodel.com** and **www.catalyst-solutions.com.au** for more templates, online assessments and other organizational change resources.

It's not working!

> A change is successful when the people involved and impacted agree the reward was worth the risk and the value created was worth the investment.

Research from Accenture's Paul Nunes and Tim Breene (2011) shows that only 7 per cent of companies which cease to grow ever manage to survive for the long term. We know from nature that just about everything needs to adapt to survive and for most organizations the aim is to do more than just survive. Commercial companies want to out-perform the competition, government and not-for-profit organizations want to provide the best services at the lowest cost. A critical area of competitive advantage nowadays is the ability of organizations to lead rather than follow changes in the market and this means having the ability to roll out the right changes quickly and reliably in a way that delivers a return on investment for the organization. Whether you are changing because you *want* to, or because you *have* to, change is difficult.

> Successful organizations actively change to better fit with their external environments. They engage in self-betterment and risk-taking in response to intensifying competition. Change is accepted as the norm (Bahrami, 1992; Claver *et al*, 1998; Denison and Mishra, 1995; Smith, 1998).

We know the facts – the rate and complexity of change in and around our organizations is increasing. What most organizations haven't yet managed to do is build the capability to respond reliably to those forces let alone stay ahead of them. We know project success rates are still disappointing and change failures continue to make the headlines. IBM's 2012 CEO survey found that 72 per cent of leaders were focused on reacting more quickly to market needs. In 2010 the same survey found that three out of the CEOs' top seven priorities related to change.[1]

It's important to begin any improvement initiative with a good understanding of where you are starting. Take a look at the assessment in Figure 1.1. The questions are based on the components that together contribute to successful change. Be brutally honest in your judgement ... if you can't find convincing evidence that the statement is true you should mark it 'false'.

Figure 1.1   Organizational change capability self-assessment

Our organization	
1 ... has a culture that helps us plan, deliver and embed change easily	True/False
2 ... provides sufficient time, people, money and resources to enable our changes to be successful	True/False
3 ... has sufficient and appropriate 'buy-in' from everyone involved in and impacted by change	True/False
4 ... has access to the capability we need to change successfully	True/False
5 ... has a clear roadmap of change aligned to our vision and strategy	True/False
6 ... effectively identifies, monitors and realizes the planned benefits from change	True/False
Our business units	
7 ... maintain the momentum behind a change – from the initial idea through to reaping the benefits	True/False
8 ... take accountability for adopting, embedding and sustaining new changes	True/False
Our projects	
9 ... reliably deliver on time, on budget and to stakeholder expectation	True/False
10 ... spend time and money making the people and the environment ready to receive the change	True/False
Total number of 'True' responses	_____

If you answered 'True' to all of the questions then you're already getting it right. The reality is that the majority of organizations score between two and four 'Trues'. No matter how your organization scored you will already be building an awareness of the diversity of components required for successful change.

It is possible our organizations used to be better at rolling out changes. There were fewer of them and so they were arguably subject to more planning and rigour. Perhaps our staff and customers had lower expectations or were more compliant. The change models of the mid-20th century talked about periods of unfreezing, transition and refreezing as if change was a one-off event that started, reached a tangible end and let everyone 'refreeze' into the new status quo.[2] By contrast, most of our organizations today change so frequently we don't really know what our 'status quo' is. We live in a constant state of flux making it hard to know where we are or which change to do next. Changes now need to be integrated into evolving organizations operating in a complex dynamic environment. Change just got harder.

Many of the costs of poor change are hidden – either accepted as a necessary evil or deliberately overlooked in an attempt to make us feel that we are doing a good job – but there are many studies which show project failure rates of around 70 per cent.[3] Whilst this figure is shocking, it is the reality of what goes on behind this revelation that is more alarming when you see the time organizations spend fixing, redirecting or re-energizing those projects that didn't deliver. There's also the change-crippling damage done by the cynicism and inertia that builds as people develop a view that nothing will ever be delivered or that changes don't deliver real business improvements. If either the change or the failure of it made the headlines there is considerable brand damage too.

It is no secret, if we choose to face it, that many organizations need to change but aren't very good at it. Despite decades of improvements in governance and project management most organizations are a long way from where they need to be. They are still wasting taxpayer or shareholder money, putting their performance at risk and upsetting their staff and customers whenever they roll out so-called improvements.

Most leaders recognize when their change attempts are in jeopardy. The three most common signs they cite are a destructive tension between those delivering the changes and those on the receiving end; unacceptable disruption to customers, staff and/or business performance; and a belief that the change delivered a poor or unknown return on investment.

The project team and the business don't get on

61 per cent of managers reported major conflicts between project and line organizations (Meskendahl *et al*, 2011).

'We asked the business what they wanted and they couldn't tell us.' It is easy to see how tension can quickly build between the project team delivering the change and the business team receiving the change. The project team are trying to build tomorrow's organization. They have been asked to do a job and can see 'the business' as getting in the way or not co-operating. They may believe they understand the business and should be able to make decisions in order to maintain progress and meet deadlines. When business consultation becomes necessary (as it inevitably does!) it is seen as a threat to the project timeline.

'The project team have no idea how we run this business.' Likewise we can see how the impacted business people can believe the project team do not have their best interests at heart. It can be overwhelming if the change feels like a steam train bearing down on startled staff and customers. The business is trying to run today's organization; their KPIs and scarce resources are fully dedicated to meeting this quarter's targets. A change that is some way off does not get much attention.

Fundamentally these two groups are driven by conflicting agendas and organizations must find ways for them to work together in harmony with common goals if the long-term benefits are to be achieved. If not addressed your project and business staff will remain demoralized; your organization will continue to produce changes that are unlikely to be accepted by those receiving them and you are unlikely to deliver any benefits.

Poor change disrupts the business

Eight out of nine teams experience a drop in productivity during times of change (Parry and Kirsch, 2011).

The second evidence commonly cited by leaders is the high level of disruption their changes are causing to customers, staff and their overall business performance. It seems obvious that changes that impact customers need special care yet many organizations still perform a cursory impact analysis and provide minimal support. Internal changes that have a negative impact on customer-fronting staff can also increase the risk of losing customers. This might be at a local level caused by a poor customer experience or across the board by creating damage to your brand.

Whether driven by curiosity or anxiety it is not unusual for staff to be distracted or disillusioned during times of change. If the change is poorly managed or the potential negative impact is significant, those who can do so easily (usually your top performers) will leave the organization. Others will reduce their productivity and make future attempts to change a lot harder. It is easy to see how business performance takes a dip during times of change. Revenues can fall and staff productivity has the potential to plummet for a long period before, during and after a poorly managed change. Sickness and staff turnover go up and employee satisfaction goes down.

The consequences of disruptive change are clear. Low productivity, staff and customer turnover are hard and expensive problems to fix. Poor business performance, combined with poor change delivery may lead your investors to lose faith and be wary about future investments. Change gets harder for organizations that have mismanaged it in the past. They are constantly faced with the cynicism, anxiety and fatigue they left behind after the last change.

Poor return on investment

> The three types of return on investment necessary to sustain successful change: financial, emotional and organizational

A group of more than 1,500 executives were asked by consulting firm McKinsey (2006) whether a recent change to their organization had resulted in improved performance; just over a third were able to say yes, a third said no or 'not sure' with the remainder saying their change initiatives were 'somewhat' successful. If you are unable to confidently answer yes to this simple question, then the change has failed. Even those who answered 'somewhat' wouldn't be providing their investors with much comfort as it is likely that these initiatives cost considerable time, money and energy and a 'somewhat' successful improvement seems inadequate.

Organizations often fail to realize the three types of return on investment necessary to sustain successful change; financial, emotional and organizational return. Poor financial return on investment means we don't achieve, or we don't know if we achieved, the value we needed in return for the money we invested. Organizations that find change difficult often do not have the skills or experience to set a realistic return on investment (ROI) and they often have no process to monitor and update this as the change progresses. We would never invest our own money the way we seem to be happy to invest our organization's money. If your financial planner offered you a product with little information about the return on that investment, you'd never buy it. Yet every day our organizations invest millions in changes for which they may never see a return.

Poor emotional return on investment means the people involved and impacted don't get the satisfaction they need in return for all the effort they put in. This leads to apathy and undermines the organization's future attempts to change. We are naturally wired to put in effort in return for a feeling of satisfaction, and successful change requires a lot of people to invest a lot of personal time and energy. In return, they expect to feel that it was worthwhile and to be proud of what they have achieved. When change is poorly managed they feel stress and resentment which once again undermines current performance as well as future attempts to change.

> Successful change moves the organization forward in the right direction.

'We didn't end up where we wanted to be and we don't know how we didn't get there.' Organizational return on investment is lost when a change does not achieve the strategic value intended and the organization does not move forward in the right direction as result of the investment. The organization doesn't deliver its strategy and customers, staff and investors become disillusioned.

The rewards for those that build strong organizational change capability are clear. Imagine working for an organization that responds quickly and easily to new opportunities and challenges; where people take on new skills and responsibilities with ease. Imagine being part of a change where you are fully engaged, involved, informed, committed and prepared; where both those delivering and those on the receiving end of a business improvement work closely together, using the best of their skills, knowledge and experience to develop the best solution with the highest chance of delivering real benefits to the organization, its staff, customers and shareholders. Imagine what is possible if people involved in and impacted by the change share a sense of meaning by being able to demonstrate a personal link to an organization's achievement: sparking a sense of satisfaction from confidently delivering a sound financial and organizational return on investment. You serve your customers better, provide an environment that attracts high-performing staff and are able to introduce business changes faster and more reliably.

So...

Before we move on to look at each of the component parts of organizational change, what are the signs coming from your organization?

1 We fully understand and deliver the *financial* return on our investment in change

Never/Sometimes/Always

2 We fully understand and deliver the *emotional* return on our investment in change

Never/Sometimes/Always

3 Our changes always achieve the *outcomes* our organization needs

Never/Sometimes/Always

4 The people delivering, leading and impacted by our changes work together collaboratively throughout

Never/Sometimes/Always

5 When we have rolled out changes in the past there has been unnecessary disruption for our ...

a Customers		Always/Sometimes/Never
b Staff		Always/Sometimes/Never
c Productivity and/or business performance		Always/Sometimes/Never

6 Given these results I think the organizational change strengths we need to maintain are...

_____

_____

_____

_____

and the weak areas we may need to look at further are...

_____

_____

_____

_____

The cycle of change

The following chapters are each dedicated to one of the elements of the Cycle of Change model. This model was developed over 30 years in corporate, government and not-for-profit organizations and has been tested on a wide range of organizational changes. It was borne out of a frustration that success rates remained disappointingly low and being involved in or impacted by change seemed as stressful as ever. Whilst most organizations were attempting to improve individual elements it was clear that most were not looking at change as a whole and were often unaware of, or were turning a blind eye to, elements that were undermining success.

Figure 2.1 Cycle of change model

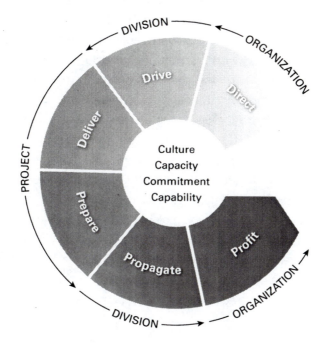

The Cycle of Change model in Figure 2.1 is a simple representation of the diverse and complex task of changing an organization and is a handy way to look at change in a holistic way. There are three areas of the model. The Cs in the middle (culture, capacity, commitment and capability) represent what an organization must *have* if it wants to change. The cycle represents the activities an organization must *do*. The Ds in the first half of the cycle (direct, drive and deliver) explain the activities that need to work together to create the right change quickly and reliably. The Ps in the second half of the cycle (prepare, propagate and profit) show what needs to be done after the change is delivered to ensure it achieves the benefits. Finally the ring around the outside reveals where the responsibility lies.

Before you embark on a change, you need to be realistic about your starting point. Given the current or potential culture, *capacity*, *commitment* and *capability* in your organization what changes can or should you attempt and when? When change initiatives are launched do they have a clear *direction*, active and energetic leadership *drive* and a reliable *delivery* method? Are the people and environment *prepared* to take on the change and *propagate* it till it delivers benefits? Finally is there a mechanism in place to ensure you ultimately *profit* from each change?

The model shows how three parts of the organization all have a role to play in making change successful. Across the organization there must be the information and processes to enable each change to have a strong direction and a way of setting, tracking and realizing worthwhile benefits. The divisions impacted by change must take an active leadership role in its development and be ready to take it on and nurture it until the benefits are realized. Finally, the people in project teams are best placed to deliver the right change and prepare the people and the environment to receive it. Only when all three groups are working together will your change succeed reliably and sustainably.

The activity components (Direct, Drive, Deliver, Prepare, Propagate and Profit) are shown serially with one coming after the other but reality is a little messier than this. We know that reliably bringing about successful change is more akin to plate spinning: no matter how well you set it up there is a need for constant vigilance and to fix flagging elements before they crash. Whilst the model will help you understand the critical activities (and you will usually start with a clear *direction*) you will find many of the activities happen iteratively and in parallel depending on your organization and the change you need to make. Figure 2.2 provides some guidance by giving an indication of

Figure 2.2 When to focus on each element

	Idea	Concept	Design	Build	Test	Implement	Embed	Sustain	Benefit
DIRECT	✓	✓	✓	✓	✓	✓	✓	✓	✓
DRIVE	✓	✓	✓	✓	✓	✓	✓	✓	✓
DELIVER		✓	✓	✓	✓	✓			
PREPARE		✓	✓	✓	✓	✓	✓		
PROPAGATE			✓	✓	✓	✓	✓	✓	
PROFIT	✓	✓	✓	✓	✓	✓	✓	✓	✓

where your focus should be at each stage. Only when you are addressing all these tasks will your change succeed reliably and sustainably.

Each of the chapters that follow provides valuable information about the 10 components. They each offer a view of the 10 most common traps that hold organizations back and the top 10 ideas that will help you improve. There are many opportunities to think about where your organization's strengths and weaknesses lie as well as tangible ways that you can improve your success rate.

For fans of John Kotter's work, Appendix 1 compares the Cycle of Change model to Kotter's eight steps and maps each of the components to those steps.

Culture to change

Culture: the ideas, customs, and social behaviour of a particular people or society

Without enough of the right cultural forces you will not deliver the benefits your organization needs.

Figure 3.1 Culture to change

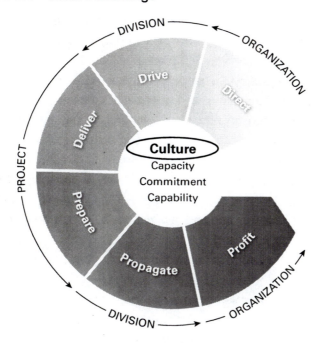

Successful organizations understand both the positive and negative forces their culture will exert on the success of their change. They adapt either the change or the culture to improve their chances of success.

Whilst some organizations manage resistance from their people during change, few look for the resistance that is ingrained in the organization. A manager once described his organization's culture as 'the stuff that's in the air conditioning and in the drinking water'. You can't see it but you know it is pervasive. You may be unaware of your organization's culture but rest assured it is exerting a considerable force on your chances of success. Its forces will have arguably the strongest influence on your ability to successfully design, implement and sustain a change within the timeline your organization needs. You must first understand the influence it is having and then act accordingly – to change it or work around it. Having a culture that predominantly supports your attempts to change is a prerequisite for success.

> 63 per cent of senior leaders said their greatest leadership challenge was 'creating an adaptive and innovative culture' (*Human Capital Magazine*, 2010)

Working in a culture that creates significant invisible obstacles and undermines attempts to improve your business can get in the way of success, no matter how smart your people and plans are. You must understand the elements that will support your change and those that will get in the way. Your plans must exploit the former and work around the latter. Organization cultures are self-perpetuating and self-reinforcing. If they are threatened they can come back twice as strong so it pays to be aware of it.

First, let's look at the difference between culture and climate. Figure 3.1.1 shows how you can think of this in the same way a sailor would check sea conditions before setting out on a journey. The climate is the part you can see – the wind direction, sun and rain; culture is the part you can't – the underlying pull of the tides and currents. Some elements of your climate may be an indication of what is below the waterline but both will have an impact on the way you approach business change.

Climate is the tone and temperature of the workplace. The dictionary defines it as 'the prevailing trend of opinion'. Think about the comments a visitor would make after spending a day in your organization: 'they were all really friendly'; 'everyone seemed very anxious'; 'the atmosphere was very relaxed' or 'everyone was so serious!'.

Figure 3.1.1   Climatic and cultural forces

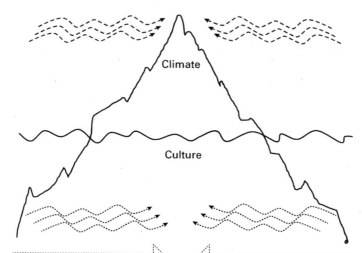

Culture is deeper and is evident in the way certain practices are maintained and rewarded. It is the signals that are sent to employees about what is important and what is expected of them. Statements like 'it is normal for managers to...', 'I am rewarded for...' or 'it is expected that...' will start to flush out some of the helpful and not so helpful elements of your culture. The comments people make will reflect their own interpretation though and it is important to find out what is behind these. It is these underlying drivers that provide insight into the right approach to take. The following statements show how it is possible to have more than one interpretation of your cultural norms.

'It is normal for all the managers to be involved in a decision which affects our department' may indicate an expectation that people will be consulted, regardless of their level in the organization, to make the best decision for the organization. This would be a helping force for change. Alternatively it may be driven by a lack of accountability – where decisions are made by committees so that no one person need be accountable. This would make change more difficult.

'It is expected that we always turn up to meetings on time' could show that respect for others' time is valued or that people are in fear of the consequences of being late from those higher up in the hierarchy. Imagine what

Figure 3.1.2   Cultural forces

Organizational cultural forces that *help* change

Personal accountability ● Collaboration ● Mutual respect ● Transparency of decision making ● High productivity ● Resilience ● Experimentation (seeing mistakes as an opportunity to learn) ● Risk-taking within limits and with accountability ● Trust ● Teamwork ● Continuous improvement ● Engaged externally ● Empowerment ● Proactive

Organizational cultural forces that *hinder* change

Independence ● Being right ● Avoidance ● Retelling of negative legends (such as previous failed or disruptive change attempts) ● 'Pulling rank' ● Internally focused ● Control ● Reactive ● Criticism ● Cynicism

it feels like to turn up late to a meeting in that organization and you will begin to see how easy it can be to identify some of the cultural elements.

'I am rewarded for rescuing projects in trouble' may mean that good project management skills are rewarded or that there is a 'hero' culture where people create poorly performing projects so that they can be seen to rescue them.

Figure 3.1.2 shows some of the typical features of an organization's culture that could be having an impact on your ability to roll out business improvements.

When you are aware of the forces of your culture you may even find yourself questioning the feasibility of the change given the strength of the forces at play. You may choose to work on improving the culture for a while before embarking on your change to give you a greater chance of success. Your organization's culture could take years to change and is largely dependent on the whims and will of its leaders. So if your timeline or remit does not allow you to alter the culture to be a perfect fit for your change, work hard up front to understand the impact it will have and design your change strategy to fit – exploiting the favourable forces and working around the negative ones.

Assess your culture

The first step is to evaluate your organization's culture, climate and subcultures and the forces at play for those people delivering, leading and receiving the change. If you have been in your organization for some time it may be difficult to articulate the elements of your culture. You will have been involved subconsciously in creating and reinforcing the norms. Start by thinking about the external influences. What rules or norms do the people delivering, leading or receiving the change bring to work with them?

External cultural forces

Factors outside your organization may not be within your control but will have a significant influence.

Geography

The culture of the country your change impacts may set the tone for involving and consulting people during your change initiative. China for example has specific expectations about the 'right' way to conduct negotiations. Deference to authority or fear of offending you could impact on your ability to obtain meaningful feedback. The case study below demonstrates how one global organization dealt with international and cross-cultural challenges.

CASE STUDY   Taylor Institutional Bank

Taylor Institutional Bank were planning to roll out a new product. The delivery team were managed from Australia where communication is relatively informal and open. The bankers that would be selling the product were spread across China, Singapore and Malaysia where employees are discouraged from exhibiting individuality and less likely to voice objections or concerns. Wisely, they worked with a specialist company to identify the norms of each geographic area and tailor their engagement and consultation approach accordingly. This enabled them to obtain reliable feedback and build the commitment they needed.

Where are each group located – in the city or a regional area? Are they in a residential, industrial, business or agricultural area? For example, people living in regional and remote areas have some unique priorities, views and assumptions compared to people living in the city.

Industry

The industry you are part of can also come with certain assumptions and 'rules'. For example, academic institutions assume that all ideas need to be analysed and critiqued thoroughly and will look for data to back up proposals. This assumption is carried into all activities and decisions regardless of the impact this may have on the outcome. If you are attempting to change an academic institution expect to engage in a lot of discussions about the relative merits of the change as well as the approach.

Profession

The profession of the people you are aiming to influence can also come with some hidden obstacles. For example, lawyers typically have an individualist culture and a tendency to look for the flaw in a plan or argument. This may help some changes but get in the way of others.

Customers

If your customers are impacted by the change you'll need to consider their cultural forces; what they value about the organization, its products and services and the assumptions they make. Their demographic will have an influence on your success; their age, location and background.

Internal cultural forces

Subcultures

Inside your organization look out for subcultures within the groups delivering or impacted by the changes. In addition to the unwritten rules dictated by the organization's culture you will often find another set of rules in use within specific areas. This may be within a function, location, department or driven by the style of a particular leader. For example the finance department is likely to have a different set of 'rules' to the sales department. A regional site may have different underlying values than those of a city-based head office. These forces can sometimes have greater influence than the overall organization's culture and will need specific plans to leverage and work with, rather than against, them.

Functions that cross the organization, such as HR, finance or risk, can provide valuable insights into the subcultures of each business unit. In order to do their job, the human resources team will have learned the rules to enable them to influence the mobile sales workforce, the customer service centre and the head office-based finance team.

Promotion

Why do people become leaders? Leaders largely create and maintain an organization's culture and the support of those leaders will be crucial to the success of the change. So it is worth gaining an understanding of what capabilities and achievements warrant promotion into these senior positions in your organization. If people are promoted for competencies and attitudes that support successful business change, such as collaboration, delivering results and inspirational leadership then you are in luck. If they are rewarded for less helpful qualities such as longevity in the organization or getting on well with the boss you may be in trouble.

New staff

The strongest elements of your culture are always obvious to someone who is new to the organization and is trying to fit in. Ask new employees what they are noticing that's different (better or worse) compared to their last employer.

Resource allocation

To find out what is really important to your organization take a look at how people spend time and money. Time and money are always in short supply and are therefore the two elements that are constantly being allocated according to priorities. Knowing what your organization sees as a priority will give you some great insights into how it will perceive your change. For example, when money is tight your organization may prioritize refurbishing retail outlets over building a new head office executive suite. This would be a good sign if your change impacts customers. Or when time is in short supply, for example in the run up to the end of the year, your organization may prioritize the completion of budget forecasts over staff appraisals. This could be bad news if your change has little tangible financial return on investment.

Communication

Your internal communication can tell you a lot about what is 'normal' in your organization. As good communication is critical to successful change – you need these rules to work in your favour. Is there a lot of two-way communication or is it all one way? Is the use of social media encouraged or highly regulated? Is the language simple or is there a lot of jargon? Who communicates? How often and about what? Has there been a change in the way the company communicates? How active and reliable are informal communication channels? Answers to these questions will help you understand the forces you are working with.

Stories

Listen out for the stories that have become legends in the organization. They usually relate to past people or events and have developed as codewords or start with 'Do you remember that time when...'. It may be a particularly good leader or perhaps a crisis. Note when these stories emerge. It could be when talking to a new employee or perhaps when a major decision is pending. Consider whether the past is referred to in terms of 'the bad old days' or 'the glory days'. The content of the story and the motive for telling it will help you uncover the mindsets you are working with.

CASE STUDY   The legend of Project Core

In the early Nineties Maxwell Bank started Project Core which was to deliver a large IT system. After a few troublesome years, the project was cancelled at enormous cost and embarrassment to the organization. The story lived on for over 10 years. It was re-told whenever a major decision was due on an IT project. Nobody wanted to risk another Project Core so decisions were delayed, accountability was unclear and it was almost impossible to roll out changes at the speed the organization needed. The legend was fuelling a culture where decisions were made by large committees after months of consultation.

Some organizations have a function dedicated to understanding and shifting the organization's culture so talk to the human resources (HR) or corporate culture team. HR teams are also often the custodians of the Employee Opinion Survey. Both the numeric data and the verbatim comments from these will give you a good indication of some of the ways in which the existing culture may help or hinder your change.

Think ...

What *external* cultural forces will we need to be aware of?

_____

_____

_____

What *internal* cultural forces will we need to be aware of?

_____

_____

_____

Culture traps

Designing a change that does not fit your organization's culture will make it difficult to deliver and sustain benefits as the invisible forces work to undermine 'the new way'. So why do we sometimes make this mistake?

Trap 1: We are blind to our culture and its influence on a successful outcome

If you have worked at your organization for more than a year you will have learned to 'fit right in'. It is likely that the elements of the culture are so 'normal' to you that you don't even notice them. (For example, it has become 'normal' to be at your desk by 7am or start meetings 10–15 minutes later than scheduled). It is therefore not surprising that we don't consciously analyse the ways in which our everyday behaviour will impact on the success of our change.

Trap 2: We are sold a vision

Often the vision of a change looks so good because it paints a picture of a world without the limitations, realities and problems of today. Of course we want that! A new system implementation will promise great management reporting, superior insights and better decisions. However, if the culture rewards emotion-driven arguments, quick decisions and low attention to detail you will never reach the vision you were sold.

Trap 3: We think it will be different for this change

We may have seen our colleagues sink up to their waists crossing a pit filled with quicksand but given the right circumstances we will still give it a go – believing that it will be different for us and we will make it to the other side. Even if we do understand how our culture will potentially lessen our chances of success, the temptation to ignore that information and keep going is overwhelming. The problems seem nebulous, too hard to tackle and outside of our control (all of which may be true). The CEO is pushing for an early delivery so we put on our blinkers and run for the finish line... all the time hoping for success despite those cultural forces.

Trap 4: We expect projects to make significant changes to the culture

We believe that by implementing a change we can influence the environment – even though that environment has been around for longer and is much stronger than your fragile new change. As an example, a consulting company with a conservative individualistic culture invested heavily in creative workspaces, open plan offices and flexible seating in the hope that their people would increase their levels of collaboration across departments and innovation in their work. The majority of leaders soon booked out the 'hot desks' and meeting rooms so their team could sit together. People seen using the creative work areas got the message that they weren't doing 'proper' work and soon felt the pressure to return to more traditional desks, equipment and meeting spaces. The planned benefits that were to come from increased collaboration and innovation were never realized – just a lot of money spent on bean bags and whiteboards and a legend of 'that crazy office idea' waiting to hamper future attempts at change.

Trap 5: We fail to align all our leaders to the new way

Project teams are rarely able to influence the range of leaders necessary or given the time to embed new behaviours prior to the implementation of a change. To bring about a change in culture a critical mass of leaders needs to behave in the new way consistently over a period of time. Leaders are notoriously hard to influence. They have come to expect greater levels of autonomy than staff at lower levels. They 'fit' with the rules, reinforce them daily, possibly benefit from them and are often the least aware of them. They may have been recruited and rewarded because they fit the old set of rules.

Trap 6: We try to change the culture and the organization together

We will need support from our managers and they are busy people. If the priorities aren't clear they are unlikely to support either initiative. When we don't understand the interdependencies between our culture and the change we can't make good decisions about the relative priorities and communicate a clear path for those involved.

Trap 7: We assume they'll do it our way

We are Head Office after all! We take the time and trouble to plan it all out for them so of course they will do it our way. Perhaps it doesn't even occur to us that they have a 'way' of their own that is different to ours.

Trap 8: We misinterpret the signs

We don't like to think there are any real obstacles in the way of our change so we take a cursory look at the signals coming from our workplace and give them the benefit of the doubt. It's great that the sales managers put so much time into managing their team members (... or is that really micro-management leading to disempowerment!).

Trap 9: We adapt the approach but not the change

We tread carefully in the way we engage and involve the people impacted. We are attentive to their needs and customs and build strong commitment as a result. They are with us on the journey but we destroy that trust by implementing a solution which clashes considerably with 'the way they do things around here' with no attempt to make the adjustments necessary.

Trap 10: We introduce cultural clashes

A sure-fire way to introduce extra tension into an organizational change is to employ an army of consultants whose culture clashes considerably with that of your organization. It is easy to do; often large consulting companies have an individualistic culture accompanied by a set of beliefs that conveys the message 'we have all the answers'. The consultants are often from academic or senior management backgrounds and have little in common with your workforce. When they come in large numbers their working practices introduce a whole new bunch of norms. These different expectations make them stand out from your team and can appear to your people to be showing disrespect for your organization's way of doing things. Your workforce cannot relate to them and don't trust them. They believe they could have done the job better (rightly or wrongly) and blame you for their disruptive presence.

Think ...

1 Which of these traps is holding back your change?

2 Which one, if you fixed it, would bring the greatest benefit?

Culture tips

Now that you have identified some of the things that may be holding you back, start doing the things that will bring you greater success. Let's look at some things you can do to improve the 'fit' of your change with the culture you have.

Idea 1: Understand the impact of your culture on your change

Work through the positive and negative forces in your organization's culture and subcultures and their relative strength. Think about their impact on the ease of the change journey, as well as support for the destination. When you start to articulate the strong elements in your organization's culture you will see that some of them will help your cause by increasing accountability and

Figure 3.1.3 Internal cultural forces in a pharmaceutical company

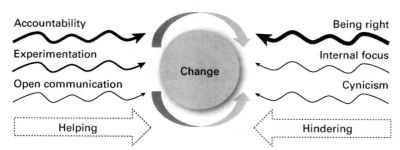

speed of response and some will get in the way by causing delays, frustration, increased risk or duplication. The assessment in Appendix 2 will help you with this.

Figure 3.1.3 shows an example of a cultural analysis for a pharmaceutical company. The thickness of the line indicates the relative strength of the norms.

You can see there are some elements that will help their change. The strong sense of accountability should make it easy to know who makes which decisions and build ownership for your change. A preference for experimentation means that they will be willing to take some of the risks required to improve the organization. However, the need for individuals to be seen as having all the answers may undermine the ability to learn from mistakes and build the organizational resilience required for successful change. Whilst the tendency to have an internal focus is not as strong as some of the other elements, if the drivers for the change are external, the tendency to look only within the organization will need to be addressed early if it not going to hamper progress.

Idea 2: Don't take evidence at face value

Work hard to understand the underlying drivers for the norms and never make assumptions. Look for the reasons and values underpinning what you observe. For example, a culture of high accountability and innovation sounds like a good thing to have when you're rolling out change. However, you will need to counterbalance this with accountability for long-term benefits to provide the staying power needed to sustain changes and realize benefits once the changes have been implemented.

Idea 3: Understand that humans are tribal animals

We are hardwired to fit in. Be realistic about the level of behaviour change you can influence and the timeframes in which you can do it. Can you build sufficient and appropriate support in the critical mass of people? What are the consequences if you don't? Does it matter? Do you need to change your approach?

Idea 4: Exploit the helpful forces

There will be elements of the culture which will help the change to be successful. Plan to exploit the most powerful elements to the fullest so they have a greater influence than the forces which may get in the way. For example, you may find a subculture that rewards experimentation and learning from mistakes. This would make an ideal team to pilot your change. If your organization has a high regard for teamwork, design your change so that tasks, goals and achievements are owned and celebrated by teams and not individuals.

Idea 5: Adopt the path of least resistance

If you need to move quickly then plan and fund the activities and approach required to exploit the strengths and avoid the dangers. Design your change and the approach so they take maximum advantage of helping forces and avoid too much damage from the hindering forces.

Idea 6: Create a subculture for your change

Assuming that most of us aren't in a position to create the ideal organizational culture before we embark on a much-needed strategic change, consider how you can create a subculture within the impacted teams that supports the change. Find ways to reward and reinforce the elements that your change needs.

Idea 7: Focus on your leaders

Articulate the change-enabling cultural elements your organization needs (such as accountability or learning from mistakes) and embed these in leadership recruitment and performance management standards and processes throughout the organization.

Idea 8: Put it in the drinking water

Everyone in the organization needs to receive a consistent and persistent message about the behaviours that are expected of them. When you have identified the cultural elements you need to support successful change, look for any structural or symbolic signs that don't support them such as collateral, resources, processes, policies or systems which send a contradictory message. For example, if you want to encourage accountability but governance processes still feel like a 'witch hunt' you'll need to align them to the new way.

Idea 9: Make cultural risks and roadblocks visible

Discuss the plan with senior leaders including allowances made for cultural obstacles. Use your change and organizational governance processes and forums to identify and discuss the risks that relate to the cultural incompatibilities.

Idea 10: Change the culture

Successful organizations understand that having a culture which is supportive of change is fundamental and will embark on a multi-year culture change programme to achieve this. In the meantime they work out ways to improve the organization and deliver its strategy within the existing culture.

Think ...

1 Which of these ideas could help your organization?

2 Which one would give you the most benefit?

So ...

Before embarking in any change journey, it's wise to get a good understanding of the forces that will impact both the journey and the destination. People delivering and leading the change must maintain the objectivity to continually identify the forces that need to be exploited or avoided in pursuit of successful change. The questions below will help you reinforce the insights from this chapter. Appendix 2 contains a detailed cultural assessment to help you. Consider asking for input from a range of different people.

1 What are the significant cultural forces that will *help* my organization change successfully?

External_____

Internal_____

2 What are the significant cultural forces that will *get in the way* of change in my organization?

External_____

Internal_____

3 How can we exploit our current culture to make our changes more successful?

_____

_____

4 What should we stop doing in our current culture that would make our changes more successful?

_____

_____

5 What can we start doing in our culture to make our changes more successful?

_____

_____

6 The most important thing I need to remember about the impact of culture on organizational change is ...

_____

_____

Want to know more?

Search engine terms: Organizational culture, organizational climate, cultural forces, leadership styles, organizational norms values and beliefs.

Capacity to change

Capacity: the amount that something can produce

Without sufficient and appropriate capacity you will not deliver the benefits your organization needs.

Figure 3.2 Capacity to change

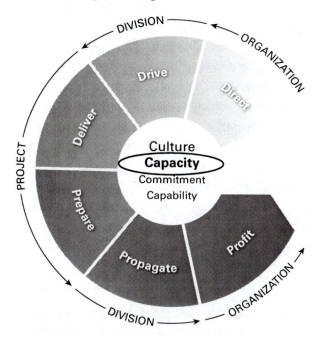

If you want to deliver worthwhile changes you'll need the people, time, money and equipment to make those changes. You'll need enough of the right *people* at the right time, *time* in your plan, *money* and *equipment* to achieve your goal.

Few people will ever feel they have all the resources they need. The reality of any change initiative is that it is competing for funds with other activities and there is a limited supply of time, money, equipment and people that has to be shared across the organization's priorities. Successful organizations manage their resources so they have enough capacity to deliver *and* receive the changes when the next initiative comes along. They don't expect to get it 100 per cent right but have processes that support the reallocation of resources quickly when priorities change.

> Change is treated as a 'when' not an 'if'.

'You can do it alongside your normal job'... 'there is no budget'... 'you still have to meet your targets'. You may have heard this before or even used some of these statements yourself. There are times when this approach is appropriate – during temporary peaks in workload or other exceptional circumstances. However, if this relates to an important change for the organization how does this manager expect to get good results... or any results? If an organization is unwilling to allocate the right resources it sends a strong message to those working on the change that it is of little value. Whilst stretch goals can be motivating, there is a point at which they can be perceived as unrealistic. When your people feel they are facing unreasonable demands or unclear priorities they become distracted – thereby reducing their capacity to take on extra or different work.[4] This inevitably leads to frustration for both the worker and the manager. Conversely, making available the right resources can improve motivation and productivity enormously thus creating extra capacity in your delivery team.

> As a leader, the act of setting aside a realistic amount of appropriate resources is an important symbol of the value the organization puts on the outcome.

It can be hard to know what you should be spending your scarce resources on. In many organizations there is a lack of transparency of the organization's priorities and its process for allocating resources. People become confused and demotivated as seemingly critical projects aren't funded and others, without a clear link to the organization's strategy, receive funding. Without a clear view of the priorities, and a transparent process for allocating or re-allocating resources accordingly, managers do not have the information they need to make the right decisions when a new change comes along.

Let's look in more detail at the resources you'll need.

People

There are three main groups of people to consider when planning access to the resources you'll need; the *delivery team* to design, build and implement the change, the *change recipients* who are the people that will be impacted by the change and the *change leaders* who will be influential in building and maintaining support for the change.

Delivery team

Making available sufficient and appropriate resources for your project delivery team is critical if you want them to perform at their best. Large changes will usually require a dedicated project team made up of a range of functional, change-management and project-management specialists. Where the organization or the change is small, people are often asked to perform a project role in addition to their usual role. This is likely to present a dilemma between the immediate priorities of today's business versus the important work required to build tomorrow's business. For this balance to work it must be possible to see how priorities, KPIs and workloads have been adjusted to accommodate the dual role.

Planning the capacity you'll need to deliver the change is relatively straightforward. The project plan of tasks, roles, timelines and dependencies coupled with some experience and a bit of contingency is a good way to estimate the resources you'll need to develop and deliver your change. Project teams will always want more resources but to perform well they must feel like they have enough to do a reasonable job.

Change recipients

Many organizations have learned to set up the project team but what is often not considered is the capacity you will need in the people impacted by the change. Most organizations go out of their way to make sure their people are fully utilized. Call-centre rosters fill each person's day down to the last minute (including bathroom breaks!), retail store staff are expected to be on the sales floor unless they are on a break. We all need time to understand, absorb and integrate new information. Giving these people the time to change means creating space in rosters and schedules and changing the rules about what is a 'valid' use of their time. They need time to be involved in the design of the change, listen to the briefings, read the communications, understand the impact, ask questions, complete the training, practice and get ready. If their days are already full when do you expect them to do this? Let's look at how Hammonds, a kitchenware retailer, approached this dilemma.

CASE STUDY　Hammonds Kitchenware

Hammonds Kitchenware had 53 retail outlets. The regional managers were focused on the day-to-day business but were becoming increasingly aware of the rate and impact of the many changes that were planned for their shops. They knew about the new EFTPOS terminals but were now becoming aware of plans to change the layout of some stores, make significant changes to the product range, change retail assistants' employment agreements and bring in a new special order procedure. They realized they didn't have a clear picture of how much change was planned for each shop or when it was coming. The head office project teams were making the decisions about implementation dates and the retail management team were beginning to feel like they were rolling with the change punches with little hope of getting up off the mat.

They soon realized they needed to play a more active role. Changes needed to be implemented when the shops were ready, not just when the project team were ready. Where possible they needed to be sequenced in a way that made it easier for staff to understand and integrate them. The impact of each change on each role had to be understood so that they could manage hotspots where multiple changes were impacting the same role at the same time. Resource plans and rosters needed to be adapted to make sure staff could be given the time they needed to prepare for and adapt to the changes.

Hammonds introduced three elements to enable them to take control of the changes impacting their teams. The first was an allowance in everyone's working week for them to learn about, train for and adapt to the changes. This sent a strong message to staff that these changes were a normal part of their role and they were expected to dedicate time to understanding and adopting them.

The second was to introduce a Change Calendar (see Figure 3.2.1) outlining common busy periods when no capacity would be available, the timing of all changes that were being rolled out, the duration of training and other preparation activities for each role.

This information enabled the leadership team to understand the impact of changes on their business and regain control. Whilst there would be subtle differences between locations, the calendar was a useful tool to help managers and project teams understand, plan and support the changes effectively.

The third initiative they introduced was the concept of 'change windows' which projects needed to book in advance. Where the change would have a significant impact, a window was also booked after the change was introduced to allow time for staff to deal with any unforeseen difficulties and get used to the new ways. For example, you can see that change capacity in November has been set aside for retail assistants to get used to the new EFTPOS terminals and deal with any teething problems.

Take a look at the Hammonds Change Calendar. If you wanted to roll out a new employment agreement for retail assistants when would be a good time to do this? If you assume the other changes are more important for the organization, February would be the earliest opportunity to implement anything that will impact on the retail assistants. Depending on the level of controversy you expect the new agreements to generate you may even want to wait until most of the shop managers are back from annual leave in March. Given that the change window for shop managers and retail supervisors is available in October you may want to use this time to consult and brief them on the changes.

Change leaders

This leads us to our next group of people who will need capacity if you want your change to succeed. The critical link between your delivery team and those on the receiving end of the change are your change leaders. They may be leading the business, sponsoring or leading the project or managing teams within the business. The research tells us that good change leadership are critical for change to be successful so they must have the time

Figure 3.2.1 Hammonds Change Calendar

	Change Capacity	September	October	November	December	January	February
Regional Manager	8 hours per week			No change: Peak period		Note: popular time for annual leave	
Shop Manager	4 hours per week	New EFTPOS terminals: briefing and planning (8 hours)		No change: Christmas and New Year Sales			Note: popular time for annual leave
Retail Supervisor	2 hours per week	New EFTPOS terminals: briefing and training (4 hours)		New EFTPOS terminals: initial operation	No change: Christmas and New Year Sales		
Retail Assistant	2 hours per week	Updated uniforms: fitting and collection (2 hours)	New EFTPOS terminals: briefing, training and implementation (12 hours)		No change: Christmas and New Year Sales		

and appropriate headspace to play their role effectively throughout. As the change progresses, managers should expect to spend considerable time understanding the impacts, being an advocate for the change and supporting their team.

Time

Understanding the time you'll need to deliver the change sustainably and the deadline you are working to will provide valuable insights. The deadline for your change may not be within your control: a regulatory deadline for example can rarely be negotiated. If the change has internal drivers you may have more control. Either way you'll need sufficient time to bring about the change sustainably within the timescales your organization needs. If the executive is not willing to face the reality of how long a change will take to deliver benefits sustainably then there are troubles ahead.

It may seem obvious but if you have less time than your change needs you'll need to deliver something different or change the deadline. Consider changing the scope of the project, prioritize the delivery of certain elements, stop or delay the project or make compromises on the quality of the outcome. All of these decisions should be made with full awareness of the potential risk to the benefits the organization needs.

Money

Your organization's resources are probably already managed through rigorous financial management and forecasting processes. Budgets are split between operating expenses which align largely to 'business as usual' activities and capital expenses which are set aside to pay for significant projects. Depending how these are formulated this could help or hinder your attempts to change. If budget forecasting encourages and supports making allowances for future activities then you are more likely to have at least some of the funding available when you need it. If these contingencies are routinely taken out before the final budgets are set then finding the money you need when you need it may prove difficult and time-consuming.

You may be hampered by a lack of flexibility in the way your organization allocates and reallocates funding. In the Hammond's Kitchenware example above, allowing time in each person's roster to prepare for changes had a knock-on effect on staffing budgets. The financial impact needed to be accommodated before they could implement the new practice. Often operational budgets can only be adjusted through lengthy approval processes. Organizations that change successfully plan contingency for change capacity in each year's budgets and have a process to dynamically reallocate or access resources as circumstances and priorities change.

Developing reasonably accurate estimates of the total cost of your change is important. Traditional project planning will tell you the resources you need to build the solution but what is often missing are the other costs associated with introducing changes into the organization such as the business team's time and any productivity impacts. If these costs are not included at the outset the related activities can be left out of plans, come as a surprise later in the project and cause delays. Worse still it can make discussions and decisions about return on investment meaningless if only part of the cost is considered. If understanding the real cost of what you want to do leads you to think differently about it then it has been a good test. Perhaps breaking the change down or approaching it differently can still meet the strategic needs of the organization but at a more acceptable cost.

To ensure you have visibility of the total cost of your change consider elements such as:

- The cost of taking people away from the business to contribute in a meaningful way to the project. For example, to pay overtime.

- The cost of having people away from their jobs to attend information sessions and training. For example, providing temporary staff to back-fill their roles.

- The extra cost of supporting the time taken for external stakeholders to familiarise themselves with the change. For example, if your change impacts customers, allow plenty of time in your plan for them to get used to the change.

- The impact on productivity and performance of any transition arrangements such as parallel running of old and new IT systems. You may need to recruit temporary staff or reduce service levels or performance targets for the transition period.

- The cost of project or business resources that will be required to monitor, refine, embed and sustain the changes after go-live.

Equipment and physical resources

The equipment you'll need will vary depending on the nature of your business and the change you have planned. You may need additional office space and IT equipment for the project team. To support communication and training you may need audio-visual equipment or software packages. If you plan to engage important external stakeholders you'll need access to high-quality venues and survey tools. If your team need somewhere to develop or test new products where will they do this?

Resource strategy

When it comes to finding sufficient and appropriate resources it is unlikely you will find them all within your organization. Successful companies plan ahead for the capacity they'll need to change and this includes having a strategy for whether they will own or access that capacity. If they decide to own the capacity this may mean having more people than they need to run today's business; leasing additional office space that today's business may not use; starting change projects early to make sure they have the time to deliver them sustainably and setting aside money to invest in the future. An alternative strategy is to enter into arrangements with other organizations that can provide the capacity you need when you need it. For example, funding from a bank loan, the use of short-term serviced offices, contracting people with specialist skills, renting equipment or outsourcing call-centre capacity.

> Resource planning is an art not a science.

There's no doubt that you'll have to make compromises. Very few companies have all the resources they'd like or can wait until all these are in place before embarking on their change. Those compromises however should be made in the full knowledge of the consequences of those decisions. If the only additional office space you can afford for your project team is on the other side of town to the impacted business teams this will have a bearing on their ability to communicate effectively and build the strong relationships required to deliver successful change.

Making the right resources available at the beginning of a change is one thing but keeping them up to date can be quite another. You will experience events as you go along that you didn't expect. These invariably cause extra cost, different skills, more man hours and/or more time. Sometimes a change in priorities within the organization will have a flow-on effect on project resources. For example, when the global financial crisis (GFC) hit in late 2008, many banks simply lacked the cash flow to support current projects and needed to amend strategic objectives and reforecast their investment to fit the new environment and available cash flow. This often meant slowing down or stopping growth initiatives and fast-tracking those with short-term financial returns. It is important to remain flexible so that you can respond effectively to new information and priorities.

Think...

1 Do our people have sufficient capacity to play their role in the change?

_____

_____

_____

2 Are financial and other resources clearly allocated in line with the priorities of our organization? If not, what impact will this have on our ability to build the capacity we need for our change?

_____

_____

_____

Capacity traps

It is likely that you have already started to identify some of the areas you have under control as well as some of the pitfalls in the way your organization manages its capacity for change. Let's take a look at some of the common beliefs and practices that hold organizations back in this area.

Trap 1: We have no idea what's coming

People's capacity for change obviously depends on what else is happening – normal business activities as well as other changes. If a team can't see what changes are heading their way they are likely to be hit by several overlapping initiatives. Without careful planning these can all arrive just when they don't have the capacity to focus on them. For example, the Hammonds Kitchenware shop staff have no capacity to take on changes in December as this is their busiest month but may have time in February. The finance department is too busy to roll out any changes around the end of the financial year but have more capacity in the second month of every quarter. Some teams may not have capacity to adopt more than one significant change at a time. Without visibility and influence over the pipeline of changes it's impossible to ensure the least disruption and the greatest success. If a change is introduced when there is insufficient capacity few benefits are delivered and staff feel ambushed thereby creating more resistance to future changes.

Trap 2: We expect a spreadsheet to tell us about our resources

Those organizations that do try to track and plan resources become dependent on the system that captures the data. Resource planning is an art not a science. Change is complex and dynamic. It is practically impossible to capture and keep up to date enough data to accurately track and plan the resources you will need. Imagine for example trying to capture and maintain accurate and reliable data on everyone's workload.

Trap 3: We turn a blind eye to reality

By ignoring the additional workload that change brings we are leaving our people to make decisions about what is important and how they should spend their time. If no direction is forthcoming they are likely to ignore the change in favour of their current role – after all that's what's in their performance targets. If this is common practice in your organization you will already be facing an increase in levels of resistance as change is associated with unreasonable demands and extra workload.

Trap 4: We think more capacity means more cost

As we will see this is not always the case. This is often a knee-jerk reaction from managers who are continually being asked to 'do more with less'. They assume that any resources required for the change must be 'additional' resources. We are often unaware of the alternatives. Creating more people capacity doesn't always mean recruiting more people.

Trap 5: We have enough resources but they are not the right ones

We have people with time to work on the change but they aren't the right people. They don't have the attributes we need. For example, bringing operational staff into project teams is a good idea but these people have often chosen operational work because it is stable and predictable. Working on a project exposes them to stressful levels of ambiguity which affects their productivity and relationships with leaders and other team members.

Trap 6: We don't have a transparent prioritization process

When managers can't see how the organization sets priorities and don't understand what is important they have no way of reliably making decisions about their resources. This can lead them to 'hedge their bets' across a range of activities of varying value to the organization. It can also lead to the creation of arbitrary rules for allocating resources: for example a 'first come first served' approach to allocating office accommodation.

Trap 7: There is insufficient flexibility

Our people, processes and systems do not enable our resources to be reallocated quickly and easily. For example, financial cycles may be annual and don't allow for transfer of funds within the financial year. Leaders may be protective of their teams and feel threatened by the prospect of transferring team members to more important work. Equipment might be managed by a central team who allocate it according to arbitrary criteria and will not consider bending or breaking those rules in the face of changing priorities.

Trap 8: We are charmed by the vision

Your CEO has engaged a large consulting company to give advice about the best structure for your organization. They come up with a model which applies up-to-date thinking and is closely aligned to your vision and strategy. On paper it looks great but when you look at the resources required to transition to that new model there are gaps. Maybe it will take more time than you have, cost more money than you can afford or require the type of people you don't have. Something will need to change before you can hope to realize that vision.

Trap 9: Our actions don't match our words

We say it is important but then we don't provide the resources to make it happen. Perhaps we don't believe it is achievable, or we think it is just a fad that will pass. Perhaps we'd like to resource it but the people and processes that control the resources won't let us. Whatever the reason, if we are not prepared to resource it we shouldn't tell people it is important.

Trap 10: We stop too soon

We make sure we have enough resources to deliver the solution. The project team have everything they need to do a good job and deliver a great solution. But nothing has been set aside for the critical phase after implementation and this can last for months. The change is fragile and needs constant attention to ensure it can be effectively embedded. Your people may need extra coaching. The solution is likely to need some 'tweaking' before the benefits can be delivered and that will all cost time and money... but you haven't got any.

Think...

1 Which of these traps is holding back your change?

2 Which one, if you fixed it, would bring the greatest benefit?

Capacity ideas

Successful companies get ready for change even when there is no change. They build, maintain and plan access to the resources they will need when the next change comes along. The good news is there are many ways to ensure you have, or have access to, sufficient and appropriate resources when you need them.

Idea 1: Expect the unexpected

Resource planning is an art not a science. You are trying to plan for an uncertain future so don't expect to get it 100 per cent right. Build flexibility into your plans and processes to allow you to dynamically reallocate resources along the way. Ensure your project governance bodies and processes assume and support dynamic reallocation of resources as the environment changes and new information becomes available.

Idea 2: Build and maintain a change calendar

Simply knowing what changes are due and when they will happen is enough for most business teams to play a more active role in preparing for those changes. At its most simple this should outline the implementation dates for each change as shown in Figure 3.2.2 below.

Figure 3.2.2   Simple change calendar

Jan	Feb	Mar	Apr	May	June
Relocation to new premises		Sales system replacement		New product launch	(Annual Performance Appraisals)

As you start to use this calendar you will find you need more information about which areas of the business are impacted by each change and you will add an analysis by department or region as in Figure 3.2.3.

You can see from this calendar that the sales department is going to be impacted by change every couple of months whereas the marketing

Figure 3.2.3 Change calendar by department

	Jan	Feb	Mar	Apr	May	June
	Relocation to new premises		Sales system replacement		New product launch	(Annual Performance Appraisals)
Sales	X		X		X	X
Marketing					X	X
Operations			X		X	X
Finance			X			X
HR	X		X			X

department won't feel any impacts till May. This is critical information to help you focus your scarce resources on the areas of greatest need.

Once you have this information you are likely to expand your calendar further to show the impacts by role of the changes and the activities required to support them (see Figure 3.2.4 below). You can see that although the finance team are impacted by the implementation of the new sales system in March, the reality is that they are busy designing, preparing for and bedding in the changes throughout the first four months of the year.

Idea 3: Develop a resource strategy

It is not realistic to expect that you will have everything you need within your organization just when you need it. Decide which resources you need to own and have ready within the organization and which you can access from elsewhere when you need them. Build relationships with the people and organizations who will be able to help you. As a normal part of business, managers should be looking for providers of people, equipment and services that will help them in times of change.

Idea 4: Fully understand the true cost of your change

Before you make most investments you work out the whole cost so that you fully understand what is involved and you are able to make a good decision about the value you need in return. When working out the true cost of your change remember to build in the cost of:

- overtime or temporary staff to backfill the people from the business that need to be involved;
- specialist skills;
- additional accommodation and equipment;
- reducing service-level agreements and performance targets during the transition period.

Idea 5: Build business time and costs into your plans

As you design and build the change, representatives of those impacted need to be involved in a meaningful way.[5] You'll need to make the time available for them to attend workshops and meetings, review documents and play an active role in the project. As you approach implementation you'll need

Figure 3.2.4 Change calendar by role

	Jan	Feb	Mar	Apr	May
	Relocation to new premises		Sales system replacement		New product launch
Sales	X		X		X
Marketing					X
Operations			X		X
Finance			X		
Finance Manager	Design the new system	Prepare for the new system	Implement the new system	Refine and embed the new system	
Accounts Supervisor	Design	Prepare	Implement	Embed	
Accounts Clerk		Prepare	Implement	Embed	
HR	X		X		

to plan for the time your people need to read and digest communications, undertake training and practice new skills. Making this visible in project and business resource plans formalizes the allocation of this time and symbolizes the essential nature of it.

Once the change is implemented you'll need to allow time for it to become integrated into daily routines. Many changes need to be refined once they are implemented. The symbolism of visibly recognizing that refining, integrating and embedding change takes time can have an extremely powerful effect on your team's confidence.

Idea 6: Change the priorities

Review all current initiatives against the strategic and operational imperatives and stop or delay some activities. Re-order the priorities within the organization such that the change becomes a 'must have' and other tasks are demoted to 'nice to have'. Make the rationale for this prioritization transparent to help managers apply this thinking in their teams. This will free up money, people and equipment to be able to focus on the most important changes.

Idea 7: Create a happy, healthy and satisfying workplace

If people are happy in their work, research from Shawn Achor author of *The Happiness Advantage*, has shown them to be around 30 per cent more productive.[6] Happy workers will apply more intellect, energy, resilience and endurance – all things you will need if you want to change your organization. Good health makes you about 50 per cent faster at completing a task. By nurturing and rewarding this attitude you can create considerable extra capacity in your team.

Idea 8: Increase staff flexibility

The broader the set of tasks your people are able to take on, the more flexibility you will have to allocate people to tasks. In their article 'Reinvent your business before it's too late', Paul Nunes and Timothy Breene (2011) suggest building surplus talent into your plans to enable people to think and look ahead. If every person in your organization is fully allocated to running today's business, who is building the business of tomorrow?

Flexibility can be an important benefit of this approach too. If your people are used to moving between different roles and working conditions they will get up to speed much quicker than someone who performs a single role. Offer your people more flexibility in their roles, working hours, location and approach and stay away from specific job titles which encourage specialization.

CASE STUDY The Bright Energy Company

The Bright Energy company had introduced a job rotation process for people in their call centre over the last two years. All their operators were given the opportunity to work across the different customer and service teams as well as in back office areas such as helpdesk and training. This was initially intended to enable them to respond to peaks in call traffic and provide cover for sick and annual leave whilst maintaining their customer service levels.

When the company was bought out by Instant Utilities it needed to move on to Instant's processes and systems. The Instant Utilities executives had a long history of staff resistance to change in their organization and anticipated similar lengthy implementation periods with considerable extra costs. As the changes were rolled out they were delighted with how easily the call-centre manager was able to dynamically allocate the team members to a range of tasks. During the system changes many of the call-centre staff were able to be involved in the design whilst also maintaining customer service levels. During implementation, only a few temporary staff were required to free up people to attend training. Rotation provided contingency and extra capacity for the organization.

Idea 9: Develop the habit of saving time and money

Between changes it can be hard to find support to 'get ready for change'. Management time in organizations is generally focused on maintaining the status quo, achieving short-term goals and solving today's problems. There can be a limited appetite among senior leaders for initiatives that create capacity that will be reinvested rather than realized. 'Spare' capacity can be seen as inefficiency and is often cut short by instructions to 'bank' it in the form of reductions to headcount or other savings.

A constant focus on increasing productivity (and therefore human, financial and equipment capacity) is possible if you encourage your people to question their day-to-day processes. Asking why they do certain tasks in a certain way can often identify a range of tasks which are either unnecessary or inefficient. Encourage your people to look for alternative solutions to problems – not just the obvious 'more time and more money'. Celebrate with your team when they identify and fix something that was holding you back. If a constant focus is unsustainable then initiate a short and sharp productivity improvement programme over a couple of weeks. Importantly keep the capacity savings ready to spend on your next change.

Idea 10: Focus leaders on capacity management

Initiate forums, processes and support mechanisms that encourage leaders to discuss and make decisions about resource allocation in line with the organization's priorities. For example, a monthly report and meeting to discuss hotspots in the change calendar and the scheduling of new change requests.

Think...

1   Which of these ideas could help your organization?

2   Which one would give you the most benefit?

So...

Before setting off confidently on your change journey it is wise to make sure that you will have sufficient and appropriate capacity in your resources to reach your goal.

Appendix 3 contains an assessment that enables you to identify gaps in capacity and the risks associated with these. In the meantime the questions below will help you identify some of the broader implications of your capacity to change.

1   In the table below answer yes or no in each section. Where you are not sure leave it blank.

Table 3.2.1 Quick capacity assessment

	To build the change	To transition to the change	To embed change
Money	Sufficient Y/N Appropriate Y/N	Sufficient Y/N Appropriate Y/N	Sufficient Y/N Appropriate Y/N
People	Sufficient Y/N Appropriate Y/N	Sufficient Y/N Appropriate Y/N	Sufficient Y/N Appropriate Y/N
Equipment	Sufficient Y/N Appropriate Y/N	Sufficient Y/N Appropriate Y/N	Sufficient Y/N Appropriate Y/N
Time	Sufficient Y/N Appropriate Y/N	Sufficient Y/N Appropriate Y/N	Sufficient Y/N Appropriate Y/N

2 Do I have enough information to make a confident assessment?
Yes/No

If 'no' what information do I need?

_____

_____

_____

_____

3 Do I have enough resources to deliver my change successfully?

_____

_____

_____

_____

4 What resource risks have I identified?

_____

_____

_____

_____

5 How can I adapt my plans to mitigate the effect of the areas which don't have sufficient and or appropriate capacity?

_____

_____

_____

_____

6 The most important thing I need to remember about the impact of _capacity_ on organizational change is ...

_____

_____

_____

_____

Want to know more?

Search engine terms: workforce planning, resource management, financial management, productivity, process improvement.

Commitment to change

Commitment: the state or quality of being dedicated to a cause, activity

Without sufficient and appropriate commitment you will not deliver the benefits your organization needs.

Figure 3.3   Commitment to change

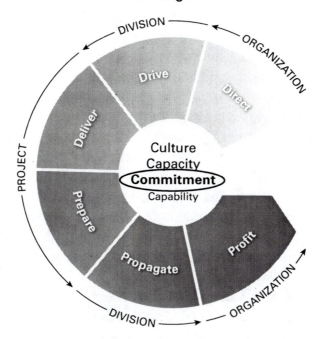

Commitment provides the fuel for change and is a powerful and versatile commodity. Having the right type and level of commitment at the right time from the right people will provide a smooth path for the change. People who are committed to the change will work harder, longer and more creatively to make it a success. With the right commitment it is possible to overcome the inevitable obstacles that change presents. The amount of energy a change requires depends on its size and how ready the people involved and impacted are to change. Our school physics lesson taught us that to shift a stationary object takes more force than to shift a moving one. If your organization hasn't changed for a while the groove it has carved out for itself will be that much deeper, the people will be more settled and you'll need that much more energy to move out of it.

When a new change gets under way the people delivering, leading and receiving the change all need to be motivated to play their part. Commitment must come initially from leaders with a strong belief that the organization needs to change. They must be the glue that binds everyone together with an unrelenting advocacy. The project team, including any vendors, must be motivated to design and build the best possible solution. The people on the receiving end of the change must be willing to be involved in a meaningful way and to put in the extra energy required to get them through the transition period. If one of these groups is not sufficiently committed when they need to play their part the success of your change is at risk.

Understanding what motivates people and what is getting in the way of their full commitment will help to develop the right approach to getting them on board. It is important to start with a good understanding of current levels of commitment. How committed are the project team to the organization and its goals? What are your stakeholders committed to and will this help or hinder your change? How committed are the vendors to the objectives of your project? What level of support is there among key leaders for the changes? How committed is the impacted workforce to the organization? This information forms a critical baseline from which to plan the right approach.

Gathering information about the level and nature of current commitment can be done through informal or formal methods. Whichever methods are used there must be a reasonable level of confidence that the results will provide accurate data that can be used to identify risks. Observation methods should focus on what people are doing rather than what they are saying to get an accurate picture. When assessing the level and nature of commitment in the delivery team and in those impacted by the changes, their manager can often provide insights into the type of work, product or customer that motivates their people. They know which tasks they tackle readily and which they hesitate to take on. They understand the activities and behaviours that are rewarded by managers and peers and will have insights into the likely barriers that will prevent their people from committing to the change. Remember though that this information will be filtered by the manager and may not be entirely accurate. They may feel they have more to lose or perhaps people are telling them what they want to hear. Bear in mind that some leaders may be poor judges of what their teams really believe.

> Leaders in particular are often well rehearsed at saying they support something when in reality they do not understand or agree with it and therefore cannot or will not support it.

For a more quantitative approach collect the data directly from stakeholders using interviews or surveys. The same filters can apply to this information too. If the organization's culture does not support open and honest communication respondents may be concerned about the motives behind the survey, the level of anonymity or the possible consequences if they provide negative responses.

Some barriers to commitment will be obvious. If it is likely that some roles will be made redundant as a result of the change there is unlikely to be a lot of commitment among the people impacted. Stakeholders' key performance indicators (KPIs) may also present an obvious barrier if they are not aligned to the change. For example, if your vendor staff's bonus is dependent on on-time delivery they are likely to put more energy into getting their component across the line on time at the expense of the quality of the solution or the relationship with your delivery team. Other barriers are a natural part of our human reaction to change and it can be relatively easy to address these. Fears driven by increasing uncertainty, perceived threats or a sense of injustice can often be addressed through strong change leadership, clear communication, support initiatives and transparent decision making.

> 'You cannot force commitment, what you can do...You nudge a little here, inspire a little there, and provide a role model.' Peter Senge (1990)

Figure 3.3.1 The path to commitment

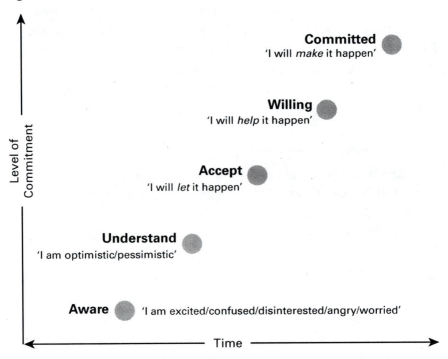

Genuine commitment builds over time. Some people commit sooner than others and some will not get there at all. It is unreasonable to expect people to truly commit to a change if they don't understand it, don't know what impact it will or might have on them and haven't had the opportunity to question it. Figure 3.3.1 shows the typical stages a person will go through before they commit (if they commit!).

For some stakeholders it may be enough for them to 'accept' the change; for others, particularly senior leaders, you will need 'commitment' if they are to be an active advocate for the change. One thing to note when looking at this model is that whilst it looks like a nice neat straight line this is often not a linear progression. The unpredictable reality of human behaviour dictates that everyone will jump around this model at different times. For example, you may believe you have 'accepted' the change but when some new information becomes available you need to go back to the 'aware' stage whilst you work out what it means to you. A constant focus on stakeholder management disciplines will ensure you fully understand the level of commitment of each of your important stakeholders.

The right level of commitment in itself may not be enough; people need to be committed to the right things. You may need them to commit to the organization, its strategy, customers, leaders and/or the change itself. For example, a company that is changing from a product-centric to customer-centric culture has, over the years, recruited and rewarded people who want to work primarily with products. These people are not easily motivated to build or work in an environment that places great customer service above great product development. They will need to manage this risk or take time to build the attitudes needed to support the change.

CASE STUDY Ivy Services

The Ivy charity provide support services for homeless people. They have a motivated workforce and high levels of staff engagement. When the Ivy Board decided to develop a commercial organization to help fund their welfare work by selling products through a retail channel they were surprised to see considerable resistance to the idea from existing staff. What they had failed to take into account was that the staff's commitment to the organization was aligned to their personal beliefs which identified strongly with the not-for-profit sector. Being associated with a commercial organization seemed to clash with these values.

In order to build the commitment needed the CEO worked hard to increase the staff's awareness of the benefits to their homeless clients and the way in which this change would secure the long-term survival of the organization. The staff were able to understand that the fundamental purpose and values of the organization had not changed and became increasingly willing to support the new direction.

Not everyone needs to be committed all the way though a change but there will be a need for a certain level and type of commitment from different groups at various points. In the early stages you need the key decision makers to understand and support the initiative. As the change progresses your focus may shift to the project delivery team who need to maintain momentum through the inevitable frustrations associated with designing and building a solution. As you approach implementation you will need to build commitment from the people impacted by the change so that they dedicate sufficient time and energy to the tasks they need to do to prepare for, adopt and embed the changes.

> Long before you need the change to stick you need the commitment to stick.

It can be relatively straightforward to build commitment in the early stages of a change project: the vision is enticing, it is new and different, the personal implications are not yet clear and the project is well resourced. As time moves on, problems are encountered, the project is delayed and it can be harder to maintain the support needed. What motivates someone in a stable environment will be different from what is needed to secure their commitment during times of change. As the change progresses, there is a need for a wider variety of approaches to build commitment from each individual. In fact, gaining and maintaining everyone's commitment to the right thing at the right time is nigh on impossible. Successful organizations secure as much commitment as is needed to keep the change moving – tipping the critical mass of people across the line to the extent that most of the others will follow and the change will deliver what the organization needs.

Think...

1 List the names of the people you need to 'make it happen'. Hint: there are likely to be less than a dozen of these.

_____

_____

_____

_____

_____

2 What are current levels of commitment? What are they committed to?

Delivery team

_____

_____

Change leaders

_____

_____

Impacted team members

_____

_____

Commitment traps

Understanding and building engagement among staff is often a constant focus for organizations but let's look at what can sometimes hold us back when it comes to building and maintaining commitment to a change.

Trap 1: We don't build on early commitment

Depending on the nature of the change and the people impacted, it is quite possible that you will have high levels of commitment early in the change. The vision paints a picture of an exciting and successful new future. As the change approaches and some of the less pleasant details become clear (long training sessions, disruptive transition periods, unintended consequences for staff or customers) we fail to leverage and reinforce some of that early euphoria.

Trap 2: We expect people to commit quickly and easily

At the outset we fail to build the level of understanding our people need if they are going to commit to the change. As leaders we often forget the journey we have been on and the time it has taken to convince *us* to support the change. When we look to build that level of commitment in our teams we forget to go back to basics, give them time to absorb the details and ask questions. Humans are hardwired to see change as a threat until they are convinced otherwise. If your staff don't know what the change is, why they need to change and what it means for them you are more likely to generate doubt, confusion and cynicism than commitment.

Trap 3: We rely on 'carrot and stick' strategies to generate commitment

These strategies, where an action attracts a reward or penalty, can provide a short-term superficial response but are not much use in complex change that needs to be sustained over a long period of time. We often use carrots and sticks to secure our children's commitment to tidying their room. We may threaten to take away privileges or offer a reward but it doesn't make them want to tidy their room every day. The same goes for building commitment to change – carrots and sticks may bring superficial compliance but in the long term are more likely to build resentment and cynicism unless supported by other mechanisms.

Trap 4: We don't know how much commitment we have

We may talk about the need for 'buy-in' but do we have an accurate picture of who has 'bought-in' and to what extent? We may be focused on building commitment among our impacted people but be completely oblivious to the level of commitment in our project delivery team. We may not be thinking about commitment levels at all on the misguided assumption that people will 'just do' whatever is required of them when we need them to.

Trap 5: We don't know how much commitment we need, when we need it or who from

It is impossible to achieve total commitment from everyone throughout the change but we often don't spend the time to work out when having sufficient and appropriate levels of commitment in specific stakeholder groups could make or break the success of our change. We stumble through reacting to the 'noise' created by someone important who doesn't seem to be 'on-board' when we need them. Perhaps they are reluctant to allocate time in their diary to meet, don't pay attention in meetings or are avoiding signing off a key document by the deadline. If we'd have thought ahead we could have answered all their questions and addressed all their concerns long before their support became critical.

Trap 6: We ignore our change history

Many organizations have change skeletons in the cupboard: projects that failed or were cancelled, changes that caused significant anxiety and disruption to employees or customers. For some reason when we kick off the next change we act as if none of this happened. As leaders we try the 'least said soonest mended' approach. A failure to acknowledge the mistakes and realities of the past quickly becomes a handbrake on our new change initiative.

Trap 7: We fail to provide consistent direction and priorities

Theresa Amabile and Steven J Kramer (2012) in their article 'How leaders kill meaning at work' use the phrase 'strategic attention deficit disorder' to explain the actions of some executive teams who appear to flip between major priorities that seem to conflict. They may appear to be focusing on a growth strategy one day and then flip to a focus on cost saving the next. They don't allow sufficient time to discover whether existing initiatives are working, and they don't communicate the rationale behind the shifts. In response to these seemingly irrational changes in direction or strategy employees learn to sit back and wait for the next big idea with an attitude of 'this too shall pass'.

Trap 8: We don't recognize or reward commitment when we have it

We may have a core group of committed stakeholders who we know will help us build the buy-in we need with the rest of the group but we take their commitment for granted. We fail to reinforce and reward it so it wanes to the point that it no longer has the power to help us that it once did.

Trap 9: We listen to what people say rather than look at what they do

The project sponsor sits at the top of the table at steering committee meetings and says all the right things: that he believes the change is critical to the organization's future and that it must be our top priority. That all sounds great, however after the meeting you find it hard to get time in his diary to meet with him, he won't approve the extra resources you need and he is clearly trying to avoid your suggestion of a discussion about the change in his next staff Q&A session. He's not committed!

Trap 10: We expect everyone to care as much as we do

We truly believe that our change is the most important thing the organization is doing right now, and it may well be. We get frustrated when others don't seem as enthusiastic as we are. We may have a lot more knowledge than they do or have had more time to consider the benefits of the change. Perhaps the impact on us personally is negligible and our work is a primary focus in our lives. Whatever the reason we build unrealistic expectations about how much commitment people will generate for a work-related change.

Think ...

1   Which of these traps is holding back your change?

2   Which one, if you fixed it, would bring the greatest benefit?

Commitment tips

It is easy to see how insufficient or inappropriate commitment can disrupt, delay or even destroy your efforts to improve the organization. It is strange then that many organizations expect their people to buy-in to the change without having specific plans in place to establish the commitment they need. Consider the ideas below and decide which can help you build the commitment needed for your change.

Idea 1: Continually build commitment to the organization and its strategy

When your people already understand the priorities and are committed to improving the organization, changes will make sense and they will find it easier to commit than if they are unaware of the bigger picture. By including this information in new staff induction processes and having a deliberate strategy to maintain and communicate it regularly the organization is becoming ready for change. If you can do this successfully, your entire workforce will be ready for the next change – already facing in the right direction with an appetite for new initiatives.

Idea 2: Understand who you need to commit, what to, when and how much

The only person who needs to be totally committed throughout the change is your business sponsor – the person who will drive the outcome from beginning to end on behalf of the organization (see Chapter 4.2). For your other stakeholders work out who really needs to be committed at each stage and focus your energy on them.

Decide the nature of the commitment you'll need. What do you need them to be committed to? You may need the steering committee members to be committed to the success of the overall organization over that of their own business unit. You may need your vendor to commit to a collaborative relationship and a shared goal. You may need the people impacted by the change to commit to a new way of working. Whatever it is you'll need to know that their commitment is helping and not hindering your change efforts.

Not every change needs the highest level of commitment. Consider the three levels from the model by Herbert Kelman (1958) outlined in Figure 3.3.2 overleaf and decide which level your change needs. This insight will help you plan the best approach to achieve the right level of commitment among the people impacted by your change.

For example, asking your team to change their e-mail signature to the new standard requires only 'compliance'. If your office is relocating to the other side of town you may need people to 'identify' more strongly with the change. An organization that is changing from a primarily product focus to a customer-centric approach needs its people to 'internalize' the change – to genuinely believe that customers are the most important element of their business. Only when they do this will their actions, reactions and decisions help to bring about and cement that change.

Idea 3: Understand your audience

Understand what they value. Each individual's perceptions, experience and personal circumstances will impact on how willing they are to commit to the change. Everyone is motivated by different things at different times and there is no substitute for getting under the skins of each of your important stakeholders and understanding what they think is important. Are they primarily driven by a commitment to the customer, the organization, their team, products or themselves? Are they motivated by money, a sense of achievement or job security? Listen to the way they talk about their work; you'll easily spot what people care about and be in a position to develop

Figure 3.3.2 Level of commitment required for different types of change

Level	Need	Length of commitment	Level of initiative required	Reinforced by	Level of commitment required
1. Compliance	'I need to be able to tell them what to do and they'll do it'	Short term	Low	Rewards and penalties	Accept
2. Identification	'I need them to understand why they need to do this and the *consequence of not changing*'	Medium term	Medium	A sense of meaning	Willing
3. Internalization	'I need them to be able to make decisions about what, why, when and how things are done'	Long term	High	Alignment to values	Committed

the most appropriate 'What's in it for me...?' (known as WIIFM) messages. Bear in mind that the majority of people will be motivated to work on whatever their boss thinks is important so maintaining commitment to the change among leaders is critical.

Understanding what your stakeholders value will help you understand what is preventing them from committing. Selling the benefits of the change is not enough. Most of us won't truly commit our energy and focus to something until we understand what the change means for us – both in terms of what we will gain and what we will (or perceive we will) lose. If your stakeholders fear losses that are more perceived than real, reframe their perspective and direct them to the facts of the change to help them. If the fears are real then acknowledge them as such so they can move forward. If you don't surface, acknowledge and realign these beliefs your change will once again feel like you've left the handbrake on.

Idea 4: Use existing data

Many organizations already measure commitment levels through annual employee opinion surveys. Check the questions in the survey and make sure they cover understanding of, and commitment to, a variety of aspects of the organization; for example brand, customer, team, leaders and strategy. A high level of commitment to customer service could get in the way of a change which is aimed at cutting front line costs. A high level of commitment to the organization's products and services could get in the way of a diversification strategy.

Idea 5: Have a plan to create and maintain the levels of commitment you'll need

When you consider that having adequate commitment to a change can make the difference between success and failure it's surprising how few projects plan specific activities to ensure they develop, monitor and maintain the commitment they need. The smart organizations decide who needs what level of commitment when, develop an understanding of each group's views and a baseline of current commitment levels and then work out what activities are required to fill the gaps. Depending on the level of commitment you need your approach to building and maintaining it in the different groups will vary. Some groups will need a short-term strategy, others, particularly those responsible for realizing benefits, will need a longer-lasting approach.

The plan should also show how you will measure and monitor commitment levels throughout the change.

Figure 3.3.3 shows the plan to build the required level of commitment from a manager, Mary Taylor, whose team will be impacted by a large system change. In a couple of months Mary will be asked to provide two of her most valuable team members to attend design workshops and the delivery team want to make sure she is willing to do this when the time comes. To focus their activities they have developed the plan below to provide Mary with the information she will need to increase her support for the change.

Idea 6: Work with your bright spots

The easiest path to successful change is always the path of least resistance. Choose areas that matter and teams that want to get involved to start the change rolling. These bright spots might be individuals, departments or customer groups. Most tasks, but especially those requiring the resilience, initiative, focus and energy that change does, are best accomplished through high-performing people. These are the people whose personal needs have been met and they are highly focused on giving others what they need.[7] Discretionary effort is an important source of energy during change so look for volunteers.[8] Think about the people who are already showing signs of commitment and are asking to be involved in your change. They are likely to be busy, curious and love a challenge. They will be naturally attracted to projects that challenge their existing capabilities and provide them with new opportunities to learn. These people are likely to be more willing than others to create the extra capacity in their day to take on additional tasks. They will be more tolerant of teething troubles too and more likely to help you fix them.

Idea 7: Build a network of powerful advocates

It is unlikely that one or two people can generate and maintain the level of commitment needed to build and deliver sustainable change. Those opposed to the change will soon rally their forces and disrupt, delay or stop the project altogether. John Kotter (1996) in his influential book, *Leading Change*, recommends building a guiding coalition to drive and support change. Spread the workload and the influence by equipping leaders with clear messages to enable them to build and maintain commitment to the change on your behalf.

Figure 3.3.3 Commitment plan for Mary Taylor

Stakeholder/ Stakeholder Group	Mary Taylor	Current level of support	Low
Commitment level required	Internalization	When (Start and end)	From early in the Build phase Ongoing
Barriers to commitment		Approach and activities to increase commitment	
1. Mary does not understand the impact of the change on her team 2. She is worried about the extra workload on her team during the transition period		1. Keep Mary fully informed as the impacts on her team become clear 2. Involve Mary in transition planning 3. Brad to meet with Mary monthly 4. Provide material to help her brief her team	

A network of change champions will also help to spread the word as the change progresses. After a series of messages from leaders most people will look to their peers to see what they think about the change. Change champions should be those people who are already committed to the change and have strong informal influence over their colleagues. Find out whose views people listen to and whose behaviour they try to emulate. Sometimes these champions will already be advocates for your change. Sometimes they may start out as your most vocal adversaries. Either way, the people who influence the way their colleagues think can be critical to building commitment in your groups.

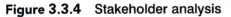

CASE STUDY   Leveraging influence

Figure 3.3.4 shows a map that was prepared for an office relocation project at Safe Ways, a health and safety consultancy. It was clear that there would be winners and losers in this change but the organization needed to build sufficient commitment to ensure that the majority of the staff would transfer to the new site. Early in the project they decided that they needed to build a strong network of support across the organization. They mapped each of their most influential stakeholders in terms of how much influence they had over views in the organization and how supportive they were of the relocation.

Figure 3.3.4   Stakeholder analysis

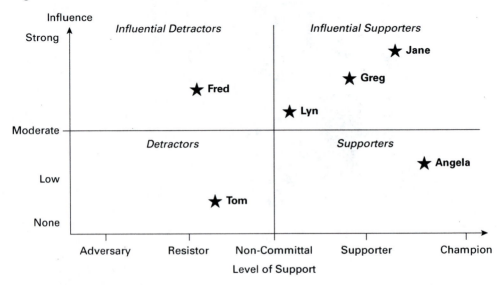

It was easy to see that Jane was ready to be an advocate for the change and that the influence she had could help sway the opinions of all the other stakeholders. They also decided that they would focus their efforts on Fred and Lyn as, if they could increase their level of support, they would have the greatest ability to reinforce positive views across the organization.

Idea 8: Communicate early, clearly and consistently

In order to commit to something you need to understand what it is and its implications. Even if the message is clear, it needs to remain consistent over a period of time and between all messengers so that your understanding is continually developed and reinforced.

Early: don't wait until you have all the answers before talking about a change. People need time to absorb information and develop their views. Set the tone for future communication by encouraging people to increase their understanding by discussing the change and asking questions.

Clearly: know your core message, communicate in plain language and check that's what they've heard. Plain language means short sentences and no company or technical jargon and no abbreviations – no matter how well you believe they are understood. The message should be able to be understood by all your staff including new team members.

Consistently: make sure the change is explained in the same way regardless of the messenger. It is hard to commit to a seemingly moving target so a message that is repeated regularly provides some certainty and stability against which to build trust and commitment. Script the 'elevator pitch' and rehearse leaders and project team members to be able to stay on message. (See Chapter 4.1)

'Elevator pitch'

The 30-second message explaining why the change is happening, why now, what is changing, when it will be happening, who is impacted and what the desired outcomes are.

The content of the message is obviously important too. Often we present the facts of a change, the numbers and business rationale. But according to Chip and Dan Heath in their book *Switch* (2010) emotional engagement is four times more valuable than rational engagement in driving employee effort so the facts alone won't build the commitment your change needs. The type of commitment and energy required to bring about organizational change needs a deeper belief that there is a benefit to doing so that your people truly care about. Appeal to their hearts not just their heads.

One of the pitfalls when communicating during change is the potential for overenthusiastic communication of the benefits of a change to the point that it sounds like 'spin' to a sceptical audience. If the benefits are not balanced with an acknowledgment of the pain and losses (however small you may believe them to be) the leader comes across as inauthentic. We are hardwired to be suspicious of anything that has to be 'sold' to us and this approach can destroy the trust necessary for successful change. Once lost it is hard to regain.

Use the right messenger to get the commitment you need. People have been proven to be nine times more likely to adopt a change if they hear about it from their line manager than from another leader. People feel their manager understands their perspective and they have a greater level of personal trust with them than with other leaders. But it's not just the manager who has the power to influence views – so do people without any formal authority. Once again you would be wise to leverage those who have informal influence too.

Idea 9: Involve those impacted by the change

Humans need autonomy – that feeling that comes when we are in control of how we achieve a task. It triggers the 'endowment effect' where the act of owning something makes it more valuable to the owner and we don't want to give it up.[9] When leaders encourage their people to take responsibility for their own reactions and take ownership of the change this can help to reduce resistance and build understanding and commitment. People who are involved in the development of changes often become its greatest advocates as they have the opportunity to build a deeper understanding of the change, its benefits and impacts. This involvement also gives them a sense of control over the outcomes.

Provide the people impacted with choices and a real ability to influence outcomes that affect them. Collaboration ranks highly in studies of commitment and helping others has been proven to be a powerful motivator. Create opportunities for impacted people to be responsible for tasks, to collaborate to make choices and support each other. Reward that involvement and responsibility so they know their efforts are valued. The extent to which this is possible will depend on the scale of change, how fast it needs to happen and the level of resistance but there should always some element of choice for those impacted.

Idea 10: Make progress visible

A sense of having made progress has been proven to be one of the most common motivators.[10] Maintaining levels of commitment necessary throughout a long change can be tough. Just knowing that you are making headway overcoming obstacles and making a difference can lead to an increased focus on and commitment to a task.

Think ...

1 Which of these ideas could help your organization?

2 Which one would give you the most benefit?

So...

Before setting off on your change journey it is wise to make sure that you have or can build sufficient and appropriate *commitment* to reach your goal.

1 What are the various groups in my organization committed to?
Delivery team:

_____

_____

_____

Vendors:

_____

_____

Influential leaders:

_____

_____

Impacted people:

_____

_____

2 Will this help or hinder my change?

_____

_____

_____

_____

3 What level of commitment does the change need?
(Level 1 Compliance, Level 2 Identification or Level 3 Internalization?)

_____

_____

_____

_____

4 Who needs to have a high level of commitment?

Now	in 3 months	in 6 months
_____	_____	_____
_____	_____	_____
_____	_____	_____
_____	_____	_____
_____	_____	_____

5　What methods will I use to measure, build and maintain levels of
commitment?
Measure:

_____

_____

_____

_____

Build:

_____

_____

_____

_____

Maintain:

_____

_____

_____

_____

6　The most important thing I need to remember about the impact of
commitment on organizational change is...

_____

_____

_____

_____

Want to know more?

Search engine terms: Motivation, power and influence, communicating change,
personal values, measuring commitment, communicating strategy, stakeholder
management, participation in change.

Capability to change

Capability: the power or ability to do something

Without sufficient and appropriate capability you will not deliver the benefits your organization needs.

Figure 3.4 Capability

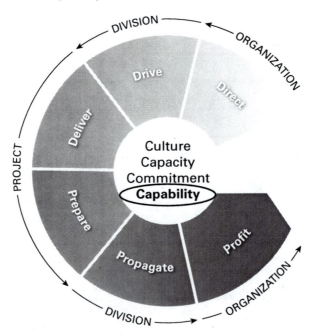

Having a great vision and strategy is one thing but as most organizations know to their cost, delivering it is a different matter. Whilst this may be for a variety of reasons the fact that they don't have access to the right knowledge and skills can be a major obstacle. Successful organizations have a long-term plan to build or access the capability they need for both the short and long term. This can include technical skills, but more importantly they focus on the core strategic capabilities that enable them to develop, deploy and integrate change over and over again, easily and quickly.

> Competence is the cumulative effect of behaviour, attitude, knowledge and skills.

Technical skills are those your organization needs to build, offer and maintain the best products and services. Your people need to be able to develop the plans, design the products, work the machines and perform the actions that make up the product or service you offer. Technical skills are a traditional focus for a significant proportion of an organization's training budget.

CASE STUDY   Mercury Bank

Mercury Bank had underinvested in their IT infrastructure over recent years. When the new CIO came in he developed an ambitious list of new initiatives aimed at updating the bank's systems. When they tried to kick off these projects it quickly became clear that the availability of some IT skills would be a constraint on what they could achieve. The talent was in short supply across the country and the cost of employing the skills needed was becoming prohibitive. They would have to cut back on the list of projects and prioritize those for which capability was available rather than those which were most important to the business.

The second group of competencies are the enabling skills; those that enable the organization to continually evolve with the minimum of cost and disruption. These are the skills an organization needs for the long term regardless of the nature or timing of individual changes. The need for these may not be as obvious and the benefits less tangible than for technical skills, particularly in the short term. However, without them an organization will struggle to bring about any of the changes it needs.

Organizational change skills

Some of these change-enabling skills are required primarily among leaders but most are needed across all levels of the organization if everyone is going to be ready to play their part in change. Organizations that want to improve their ability to adapt should focus on building and maintaining the following areas of capability.

Learn

The future for an organization is full of new and different risks and opportunities. If an organization thinks it already has all the answers then it is in for some surprises. Organizations that can change easily learn from their own experiences and those of others. They expect to adapt, adopt or avoid those lessons and continually improve the way they manage their business as a result.

> 'In times of change, *learners* inherit the Earth, while the *learned* find themselves beautifully equipped to deal with a world that no longer exists.'
>
> Eric Hoffer[11]

Monitor the environment

This is the ability to continually scan the external and internal environment for changes, opportunities and risks, assimilate new information and understand its consequences for the performance of the organization. As Jack Welch the ex-CEO of GM said, 'If the rate of change outside the organization is greater than the rate of change inside the organization, the end is nigh'.[12] Kodak the film maker did not survive in part because it failed to respond quickly and effectively to changes in technology and consumer habits. Many newspaper companies are struggling to find a new business model in the face of rapidly declining newspaper readership and free access to internet news services. Being able to predict trends and make incremental adjustments ahead of any major events maintains performance and reduces the costs and disruption of having to respond to a crisis later. As new information becomes available an organization needs to be able to decide what they will and won't respond to, adapting their strategy when required and understanding the consequences.

Communicate a clear direction

There are several skills implicit in this activity. Being able to confidently make decisions about the organization's vision and strategy is critical. If the workforce is expected to follow they must know where they are going. When the direction is decided you will need the ability to clearly and consistently communicate that direction in a way that allows leaders to communicate authentically while maintaining the integrity of the message. As changes in direction are decided you must have the capability in your people and processes to clearly articulate the new direction, the rationale for the decision and what you need them to do as a result.

Manage complexity

This is the ability to effectively manage a complex web of information, dependencies, activities and resources. There is already a lot to keep track of when making decisions and managing a business; factors inside and outside of the organization and industry; past, present and future considerations and balancing the needs of a variety of potentially conflicting stakeholder interests all come into play. Changes need to be integrated quickly so the organization can move on. Organizations must be able to manage this complexity effectively so they fully understand the consequences of their decisions and actions. If this ability is lacking they quickly become overwhelmed and ineffective.

'Organizations which master basic disciplines will excel – being able to adapt and grow is one such basic discipline.'

(Senge, 1999)

Be flexible

Flexibility is having the ability to easily change what people do and how they do it across the whole workforce – including senior leaders. Flexibility is not a skill that can be taught in the classroom but it is a capability that can be developed in the people within an organization. By recruiting people who are open to new opportunities and frequently offering them the chance to improve or change what they do or how they do it, they will be ready to change when you need them to. A significant organizational shift will be reliant on senior leaders to change their approach and they should not be immune from the need to be flexible.

Be resilient

Individuals and the organization as a whole need to build the ability to bounce back from adversity and move on quickly. Growing a business means taking risks and not all these risks will pay off. Your people, processes and systems must be able to limit the damage done by problems and obstacles. The ability to recover quickly will increase resilience with every change.

Lead change

Managers must be able to lead people effectively through changes. Whilst some organizations invest in management training, few understand the need to develop the specific leadership skills needed during change. Managers are usually recruited and rewarded for maintaining the status quo. They are often ill equipped to deal with the challenges that leading change brings. They need to be able to manage their own reaction and that of their team, deal with uncertainty, manage the extra workload and impacts, communicate effectively, reinforce and integrate changes and be a good advocate throughout. Managers need to be able to confidently lead their team into the relative unknown.

Manage emotions

We are hardwired to resist change. Just knowing that these emotions are a normal part of the change landscape can go a long way to maintaining momentum and business performance during times of change. Organizations that continually evolve realize these reactions are normal. They expect to see various degrees of shock, anger and resistance and provide their people with the tools and support to manage them quickly and effectively so that both they and the change can keep moving.

Deliver reliably

The ability to deliver the right outcome on time and to a budget enables the reliable design and delivery of changes – whatever they may be. Planning, change management and project management skills are often only considered in the context of large projects but the reality is that this capability should be continually available to the organization. A good project manager will play a key role in ensuring that changes are well planned, designed and executed with the minimum of surprises (see Chapter 4.3 for more on this). A good change manager will make sure that the solution 'fits' the business and that everyone is ready to take it on (see Chapter 4.4 for more on this). More generally, the ability to estimate, plan and work as a team to deliver a goal to a deadline are skills that are valuable across the organization.

Change capability and competitive advantage

'The only sustainable competitive advantage is an organization's ability to learn faster than the competition.' (Peter Senge, 1990)

Consider the relative value of technical and enabling skills in terms of competitive advantage. Whilst technical skills may be the easiest to define and the quickest to achieve they are also the easiest and quickest for your competitors to copy and the first to become obsolete. As the rate of technology and other change increases, the ability of an organization to own the right technical skills when it needs them has been under significant pressure. Even universities are struggling as some course material becomes out of date before or soon after students graduate. Rapidly changing technical skills are being seen as less of a competitive advantage as they become harder to keep up to date.

CASE STUDY   Manning & Partners

Manning & Partners Architects had already been through a lot of change and knew there was more to come. The last of these had caused so much disruption that two of their large clients had taken their work to a competitor. They decided they needed to build their capability to change more quickly, easily and with less upheaval to their staff and clients than previous changes had caused.

Over a period of two years they helped their people become masters of change; equipping them with the tools, processes, knowledge and skills they would need. In addition to the plan for the organization as a whole they developed a specific programme for managers to help them develop and reward change capability in their teams.

When a major restructure was announced everyone was able to understand and perform their role quickly and effectively. The restructure went smoothly and was completed in record time. All client deadlines were met during the transition period and the benefits were delivered early.

They now see each change as an opportunity to build and maintain this capability – a sort of real life case study. Every change leaves them with increased change capability and makes them even more ready for the next exciting challenge.

The competencies that enable successful change whilst harder to achieve are almost impossible to copy. Building capability in *how* your organization does things as well as in *what* they do is a good complementary long-term strategy. Having a large part of your workforce able to design, deploy and adopt new ways of working, effectively manage their own emotional reactions and those of their colleagues and customers, is capability that will be useful to the organization for many years.

Capability strategy

For an organization to increase its ability to change it must have a clear strategy to own or access the capability it needs now and in the future. The 1990s and early 2000s saw many organizations turn to outsourcing as a way of access-ing the technical skills they needed. More recently offshoring to countries such as the Philippines and India has been a common strategy as demand has outstripped supply in home markets, technology has improved and a lower-cost well-qualified workforce has become available elsewhere. The decision to access capability from outside of the organization, ie buy it in when it is needed rather than build it in-house, is often taken for short-term reasons. Outsourcing or offshoring can be seen as stand-alone cost-saving initiatives. However, if it is considered as part of the organization's capability strategy it is possible to avoid some of the common pitfalls of this type of arrangement.

The decision to build or buy capability will never be clear cut. There is inevitable uncertainty involved in making predictions about the future. The strategy should therefore focus on the skills that will support a wide range of technology, customer or market trends. As we have seen, capability that can be considered for access from outside the organization includes anything that is easy for your competitors to copy, skills that are only required in the short term, those that are likely to become redundant in the short to medium term or those that can be accessed from the same suppliers as your com-petitors with little or no impact on your competitive advantage. Capability you need to maintain, develop and own in-house includes any important skills with longer-term value, anything that is critical to your competitive advantage and those that are difficult for your competitors to copy.

A hybrid approach is to use skills available externally to build internal capability when you need it for example from vendors, consulting companies or specialists. This approach helps when you need to start work on a change but do not have all the capability you need in-house. This is a valid approach if it is driven within the context of a capability strategy. If these skills will be required over the medium to long term it is possible to arrange for external parties to build the capability in the permanent workforce as part of their assignment. Another approach to this same strategy is to recruit a tranche of people with the new competencies required into the organization. For example, a large transformation programme may result in a new leadership team who have the attributes the organization needs. They can then fast-track the development of these competencies in their teams. Figure 3.4.1 below shows a summary of which capability is appropriate to each approach.

Making sure you have what you need when you need it requires a long-term strategic plan for recruitment and people development. It may mean

Figure 3.4.1 Capability sourcing

	Develop in-house	Buy in when required	Buy in and transfer capability
Suitable capability	Capability which: • is required over a long period • will remain consistent over time • is critical to competitive advantage • enables success in a range of areas	Capability which: • can be accessed elsewhere when required • is not critical to competitive advantage • becomes out-dated quickly • is easily copied by others • is not economical to retain in the organization in the volume required • is required for a short period	Capability which: • can be accessed elsewhere when required • can be transferred successfully into the workforce within the time required • has recently been identified as important but which there has not been time to build
Example	Flexibility, Change Leadership	Java programming	Project Management

developing skills and knowledge that have little relevance for the organization of today.[13] Its benefit is in the future; it makes you ready to adapt and deliver success in your future organization. This can often be too intangible for the CFO when it comes to budget time and long-term people planning is often an early victim of budget cuts. Getting the balance right requires the human resources department to work strategically with business leaders. HR can support the identification, building and maintenance of organizational capabilities but ultimately it is the business leaders who need to see the value of this capability and remain committed over a long period to building what the business needs.

Figure 3.4.2 shows the capability strategy for a large media company. It shows how the skills related to legacy equipment like tape operation are only required for the next couple of years and will need to be carefully transitioned out. To be able to compete effectively in the fast-changing media industry they have identified flexibility as a capability they need to build in-house and have decided that job rotation is a good way to overcome the legacy of highly specialized roles and start to build the flexibility they need.

Think...

1 Which of the change-enabling capabilities do I think my organization does well?

_____

_____

_____

_____

2 How would I describe my organization's current approach to planning, building and maintaining the capability we need now and in the future?

_____

_____

_____

_____

Figure 3.4.2 Capability strategy

Have	Need	Dur'n	Core (in-house)	Non-core (buy/hire)	Transition out	Maintain	Build/buy	Plan
Non-technical capability								
Leadership		5yrs+	✓			✓		Maintain current leadership development programme
	Flexibility	5yrs+	✓				✓	Introduce job rotation for all levels
	Change leadership	5yrs+	✓				✓	Provide training for all people leaders and 1:1 coaching during changes
	Monitor environment	5yrs+	✓				✓	Transition from external consultant led to internal strategy team led
Technical capability								
Tape operation		2yrs	✓		✓			Offer career transition support to tape operators
Tape maintenance		2yrs		✓	✓			Consider outsourcing
Media system operation		5yrs+	✓			✓		Continue to offer training, support and reinforcement of best practice
IT desktop support		5yrs+		✓			✓	Consider outsourcing
Project Management		5yrs+					✓	Hire in and transfer skills to meet needs of project schedule

Capability traps

It is clear to see how the right capability available at the right time helps change initiatives run smoothly. So let's look at some of the reasons we often do not have the capability we need.

Trap 1: We don't plan ahead for the skills we'll need in the future

Most organizations forecast how much money, real estate and IT capacity they will need but not the capability. When they need to change they are often faced with legacy skills the organization no longer needs and a long and expensive journey to build or access the skills they need to deliver the new strategy.

Trap 2: We only focus on technical skills

We bring in additional call-centre operators to deal with new customer enquiries and teach them to follow the scripts and use the systems required to do the job today. We overlook the other critical capabilities that we will expect from our people as soon as they are impacted by a change like flexibility and resilience. Our management training teaches how to manage in a relatively stable environment and we are then surprised when leaders seem to struggle to manage themselves and their teams effectively during change.

Trap 3: We assume that everyone is ready, willing and able to learn new skills

Most people's skills are a core part of their identity and in many cases are a critical part of what makes them feel important at work. Acknowledging that these skills may no longer be valued can be a tough adjustment. On top of this, learning new skills is fraught with fears about whether they will be competent and how quickly they will be able to regain their 'expert' status in the eyes of their colleagues. All of these forces will be holding you back if they are not adequately acknowledged and addressed.

> 70 per cent of respondents cited 'recruiting and retaining key talent' as their current leadership challenge (*Human Capital Magazine*, 2010)

Trap 4: We assume we will have time to train people

This may have been the case a few years ago. We could see changes coming for a while before they happened and those changes were reasonably simple. Now that most changes are more complex and unpredictable, and the skills needed more dynamic, a different approach is needed. The non-technical skills required for change often need to be recruited, built and reinforced by leaders over a long period before they can be relied upon to support a change. A simple training course on the topic of resilience is unlikely in itself to produce a resilient workforce!

Trap 5: We waste the capability we build during change

Large projects are often an opportunity to build capability in important areas. Funding is made available, specialists in organizational change or project management are brought in, training is offered, toolkits and methodologies are developed – all of which provide a firm foundation for an organization to change. However, when the project ends and the funding stops many of those people will leave the organization in search of their next big challenge and toolkits will collect dust in someone's bottom drawer. When the next change starts there is often little legacy capability and we are forced to build it again from scratch wasting valuable time, energy and money in doing so.

Trap 6: We confuse capability with commitment

So are they unable or just unwilling? Managers can often make assumptions about why capability is not available within the team. Training is seen as the magic bullet which can give you what you need overnight. 'Send them on a training course' is a common cry from managers who want their people to demonstrate less resistance to change. Training makes it someone else's problem. Acknowledging that their people are not motivated means it's the manager's problem. If people are unwilling to be more flexible then all the training in the world won't improve that capability.

> Capability and commitment are closely linked. A lesser skilled person can perform better than a person of greater skill if the lesser skilled person is more committed to the outcome.

Trap 7: We think leading change is the same as leading 'business as usual'

Many managers never have any training to be a manager and yet they are required to lead a diverse group of unpredictable human beings and deliver what the organization needs. Nothing makes those people more unpredictable than change and many managers are caught off-guard as they and their people start to react in a way they have never seen before. They attempt to manage them with the strategies that have worked in the past and find they don't work.

Trap 8: We overestimate our organization's abilities

It is normal for us to be a little overconfident about our knowledge and abilities (Roxburgh, 2003). Various studies have reported that 95 per cent of professors believe they are above average teachers and 93 per cent of people say they are above-average drivers! Leaders have been shown to be at least 20 per cent more optimistic in their views than their team members on a range of assessments. The truth is we often do not have enough knowledge, experience or objective measures to know the truth. It is possible that your organization is more agile than your competition... but it is also possible that it is not and the consequences of hubris could be fatal for your organization.

Trap 9: We underestimate the capability we'll need

This is understandable. The change is new, it's something your organization hasn't done before so it's natural that you won't have a clear view of what you'll need. Often though we are unaware of how inaccurate our planning is and how much capability may be missing until it starts to have an impact on our ability to lead, deliver, adopt or embed the change. At this point it inevitably adds cost and delays our benefits until we can find a solution.

Trap 10: We put our *available* people to work on the change not our *best* people

Building the new organization should be an exciting challenge and a reward given to those who have shown the skills and attributes required to operate in this challenging environment. These are often our top performers. Instead we worry that they are too critical to today's operations or underestimate the power of the enabling skills and instead find others with purely the technical skills to get the job done.

Think...

1   Which of these traps is holding back your change?

2   Which one, if you fixed it, would bring the greatest benefit?

Capability tips

So now you have identified some of the things holding you back. What can you do to help you build the capability you need to change successfully?

Idea 1: Leverage the capability you have

Change is always easier if it uses technical and non-technical skills and competencies that are readily available in the organization. Raising awareness of the capability you already have can lead to you altering the vision of, or approach to, your change. For example, when cheap imported clothing started to become available, a sewing machine manufacturer might predict that people would stop making their own clothes and demand for sewing machines would decline rapidly. It could look inside the organization and identify a strong capability to 'make precision mechanical equipment'. Over a relatively short period of time they could make the shift from sewing machines to other equipment and continue to be successful. Asking your staff, customers and competitors what the organization is good at will elicit some insightful data from which to start your planning.

Idea 2: Identify the capability you'll need

Whilst this may involve an element of crystal ball gazing it is a worthwhile exercise to look at what you want the business to achieve in the future and articulate the capability required to achieve those goals. Look at your business strategy to identify the capability you'll need and how long you'll need it for. Make sure you think about technical *and* enabling capability – *what* you'll need to be able to do as well as *how* you'll need to be able to do it.

Idea 3: Develop a strategy to build the capability you'll need

You'll need a strategy to guide whether you will build or buy the capability you need now and in the future. It must include a transition plan for redundant skills and the approach to strengthening existing capability as well as a plan to build new skills. Then decide which you need to have in-house and which you can access from outside of the organization and use this information to decide whether to build it, buy or hire it in. Figure 3.4.3 provides a suggested planning template which is also available in Appendix 5. Use the information in Figure 3.4.2 to help you.

Finally, develop a plan to ensure that:

- redundant capabilities are transitioned out in a way that does not impact on performance or your people's dignity;
- the development of core capabilities are supported by a sound sustainable programme of development and maintenance; and
- reliable sources are identified for accessing capability externally.

Idea 4: Create the right environment

Introducing new capability is a change in itself and should be treated as such. Before you set out you'll need to prepare the way by removing the things that will get in the way and providing support for the things that will help you achieve your goals. For example, if you want to build flexibility in your workforce but HR policies and employment contracts enforce rigid rules then these will need to change first. If you want to improve your ability to use information from outside the organization but the culture only respects internal sources you'll need to address this. If you need your leaders to reward emotional self-management skills within their teams they will need practical help to know what to look for. Be realistic about what you can achieve in a limited timeframe given the entrenched forces you will encounter in your organization.

Idea 5: Differentiate between training and learning

Understanding the difference between training, as a time-bound endeavour, and learning as a continual activity will create the right mindset for building what you need. Your people should be encouraged to learn from every opportunity. This approach will also help to assign responsibility to the most

Figure 3.4.3 Capability strategy

Have	Need	Dur'n	Core (in-house)	Non-core (buy/hire)	Transition out	Maintain	Build/buy	Plan
Non-technical capability								
Technical capability								

appropriate leaders, clearly articulate the behaviours you need to see and develop appropriate measurement systems.

Idea 6: Invest in building change-enabling capability in everyone

If the whole organization needs to change then the whole organization needs the capability to change. Discussions about building capability can quickly become an 'us and them' approach with senior leaders deciding what capability they need in their teams. Leaders' needs are somehow excluded from the conversation. Some employees may also be assumed to be out of scope for skills development such as those approaching retirement and casual temporary or part-time workers. Vendors or other business partners that you rely on heavily are traditionally not included in this type of activity. For every person involved in your organization's success that does not have the capability you need that is another foot on the brake for your change. If it is the leaders that don't have what you need then it is the equivalent of another pull on the handbrake. Make sure your strategy covers everyone involved in your organization's success.

Leaders are not immune from the need to build flexibility and resilience.

Idea 7: Take a long-term view

Big change programmes are often a great opportunity for organizations to build change and change management capability. There are new challenges to be overcome, funding is available and there is a burning platform to drive it. Skills, processes and toolkits are developed and begin to get a foothold just as the programme is winding up. Now is the time to protect and nurture this capability so that it is ready to access when you next need it. Ensure the skills and tools are handed over to the business and integrated into their way of working. It may be inevitable that some of the skills will be lost but you should always aim to have greater capability in the organization at the end of a change than you did at the beginning.

CASE STUDY   Harraps Engineering

Harraps engineering company had rolled out two large change programmes over the last seven years. Each time they brought in change and project management experts to help them. These experts brought with them great tools, skills and processes but there was no expectation that the organization would adopt any of this capability. External experts were relied upon throughout, with employees playing a relatively passive role. Skills, toolkits and processes were lost when the external experts left at the end of each programme.

As the latest transformation programme kicked off it became clear that once again it would be reliant on costly external experts and would need a long ramp-up period before the change could start. This time the CEO made it clear that the company needed to take a smarter approach. He assigned responsibility for building a specific in-house capability area to each of the executives. The CFO was responsible for establishing project finance capability. The COO was asked to build project management and governance capability. The business unit executives were held accountable for building change leadership and flexibility in their teams through the opportunities provided by the programme.

The CEO monitored the progress of this initiative. By the end of the programme they had built sufficient capability to enable them to manage more improvement initiatives in-house. They were also much better equipped to start the next big change programme – with people processes and tools ready to ramp up quickly.

Idea 8: Practise and be persistent

Your mum was right – if you want to do something really well you have to practice. The work of Anders Ericsson, found that most people who gain mastery in any field have practised it for at least 10,000 hours (5 years of working hours!) (Ericsson, Prietula and Cokely, 2007). Most changes can't wait that long but it reinforces the need to provide people with frequent opportunities to apply the new knowledge and practice their new skills in the course of their working day. Learning about flexibility in the classroom is a good start but your people won't become more flexible until they have had several opportunities to try it. Maintaining the focus required to build and maintain new capability requires a long-term view of the return on investment.

Idea 9: Stay flexible

Just like capacity, having the right capability when you need it can be more of an art than a science so you'll need to frequently review your strategy and make adjustments as you go. Skills you thought would be redundant may be required for longer than you thought. If your original plan is not giving you what you need when you need it you should change your approach.

Idea 10: Buy an organization that has the capability you need!

This is not an option for everyone but it should certainly be considered. Given the right target and a merger process that enables capability to flourish this can be a quick way of developing the agility you need. eBay's acquisitions for example are guided by three principles, one of which is that the acquired company brings with it a key capability that the organization needs to deliver its strategy.[14]

Think...

1 Which of these ideas could help your organization?

2 Which one would give you the most benefit?

So...

Before setting off on your change journey it is wise to make sure that you have sufficient and appropriate capability to reach your goal. The template in Appendix 5 will help you articulate your capability strategy when you are clear about what you have and what you need. The following questions will help you with this step.

1 Which *change-enabling* capabilities does my organization have and what do we need?

	Have now	Need in the next 3 years
Change deliverers:	_____	_____
	_____	_____
	_____	_____
Influential leaders:	_____	_____
	_____	_____
	_____	_____
Our people:	_____	_____
	_____	_____
	_____	_____
Vendors:	_____	_____
	_____	_____
	_____	_____

2 Which *technical* capabilities does my organization have and what do we need?

	Have now	Need in the next 3 years
Change deliverers:	_____	_____
	_____	_____
	_____	_____
Influential leaders:	_____	_____
	_____	_____
	_____	_____
Our people:	_____	_____
	_____	_____
	_____	_____
Vendors:	_____	_____
	_____	_____
	_____	_____

3 What capability do we have that is only required for the short term?

_____

_____

_____

_____

4 What capability do we have that is no longer utilized?

_____

_____

_____

_____

5 Are there opportunities to change the way we source some capability? Non-technical capability:

_____

_____

_____

Technical capability:

_____

_____

_____

6 The most important thing I need to remember about the impact of _capability_ on organizational change is ...

_____

_____

_____

_____

Want to know more?

Search engine terms: skills audit, soft skills, competitive advantage, organizational capability, skills planning, resource management, workforce planning.

Direct
the change

Direct: to channel or focus towards a given result

Without the right direction you will not deliver the benefits your organization needs.

Figure 4.1   Direct

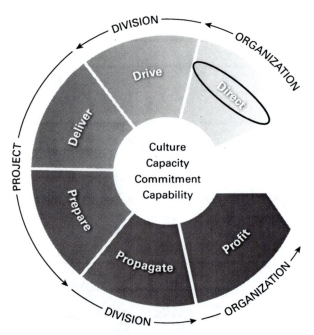

Successful organizations *direct* change. They clearly articulate the direction, the destination and the path to get there. Everyone in the organization has the same clear picture of where they are going; they know how to get there and they believe it is achievable. Within each change initiative everyone is focused on the same goal and is working confidently towards it. Clear direction focuses energy, makes the best use of resources and optimizes productivity. *Directing* change means having a clear view of the problem or opportunity you are addressing, the outcomes you need to achieve by when and how these fit into the bigger picture.

Improvement always means change but change doesn't always mean improvement. Successful organizations move forward in the right direction. This simple statement contains three important words: 'moves' assumes your organization is changing not staying the same; 'forward' implies these changes are improving your organization not making it worse; and 'direction' says you know where you are heading even if you are not entirely clear on the destination. Some organizations change but seem to end up the same: a disjointed array of projects are carried out, some of which seem to contradict each other. Their people feel like they are going round in circles as many changes don't deliver any tangible benefit or sense of progress.

Moving in the wrong direction, different directions or not knowing in what direction you are heading will waste valuable resources and at worst cost your organization its life. A study of junior managers by LIW (2009) identified 'defining organizational direction' as their biggest challenge. This would seem to indicate that either there is no direction or that it is not effectively communicated. Having a clear and achievable direction for the organization makes it a lot easier to invest confidently and make decisions that will deliver the progress your organization needs.

So before setting out on a big change journey people need answers to some basic questions for both the organization as a whole and for the individual change initiative you are asking them to support:

- Where are we going?
- Why are we going there and why now?
- How will we get there?
- What changes will we make?

Where are we going?

'If you don't know where you're going you'll end up some place else'
(Yogi Berra).[15]

Directing the organization

The context for your change is critically important – both to build understanding and to ensure it is addressing the organization's priorities. A few years ago organizations had a vision with a 5- to 10-year time horizon. Over recent years it has become evident that accurately predicting the future is becoming more difficult. Many companies have abandoned their long-term vision as it becomes clear that either the destination or the timeline is no longer appropriate. In response to this two things have happened. Firstly, organizations are setting short-term horizons – maybe two to three years. Their goals may be a step on the way to a longer-term vision but it is the short- to medium-term goal that is used to define and motivate programmes of work. There has also been a move away from the multi-year change project where little benefit was delivered in the early years. Changes are increasingly being managed through flexible strategic portfolios of smaller short-term projects which aim to deliver important benefits quickly. It is easy to see how being change-ready is critical if an organization needs to take this nimble approach. People, processes and systems need to become more agile so that you can ramp up projects and deliver sustainable benefits quickly.

In Chapter 3.4 we saw that one of the important change-enabling capabilities for an organization is to be able to continually scan the environment for new information then use this data to validate or realign direction. The example below shows how this approach influenced the direction set by a bank throughout the 2000s.

CASE STUDY   Articulating the company vision

Coleridge Retail Bank had always set a clear vision to motivate its staff. The vision was used to prioritize investment and help managers make good decisions about what to work on. Here's how that vision changed over the years.

'The Best Customer Service' (2000)

As they improved their customer service scores, so did their competitors, so they remained in third place for several years. The vision was looking unattainable and so provided less motivation than it once had. Whilst customer service scores had improved, competitors were better placed to reap the rewards from the increasing property boom and customers were increasingly moving their banking to their mortgage provider. They took the decision to react to this trend by changing the vision to be ...

'No. 3 for mortgages' (2005)

They had fallen so far behind the market leaders that getting to No. 1 was considered unachievable so they aimed for No. 3. This singular product focus worked well and drove a significant improvement in mortgage as well as day-to-day banking market share. Then in 2008 the global financial crisis hit out of the blue and the demand for mortgages reduced significantly. At the same time it became clear that the crisis would have a long-term impact on their ability to obtain funding. They quickly shifted their focus to bringing in cash deposits and changed their vision to ...

'Double our deposits' (2009)

The changes in direction seem sensible and show a willingness to respond to new information. All these goals were achievable and anyone implementing or impacted by change in this organization always had a clear direction on which to anchor or question their initiative.

It is easy to see, though, how disciplined communication is critical to retaining confidence in a changing vision. In this example it is possible that, without careful communication of the rationale behind each change in direction, staff would become confused and initiatives would stall. A change in direction is like any other change. It must be supported by information about the rationale, an explanation of why the previous direction is no longer appropriate and why the new one is the best one. Only then can staff assess the impact on their work, make appropriate decisions and reset their commitment to the new goal.

The second exciting, but slightly unsettling, change to come out of the trend away from longer-term planning is the concept that it is okay for an organization *not* to have a clear view of where it is heading in the long term. It has only a foggy vision of the future and uses short-term visions and change projects to help explore possibilities. Given the uncertain future that many organizations expect this seems like a sensible strategy. There is more confidence in short-term goals and benefits and the organization is better able to change direction if it has not committed to a long-term path. There are some attributes, however, that need to be developed within the organization to support this approach. As we saw in Chapter 3.3 people are more likely to commit to a change, and therefore give it the energy and attention you need, if they fully understand it, have a clear picture of what it will look like and understand the impact on them. Given that humans are somewhat hardwired to fear uncertainty, unclear or incomplete visions make commitment difficult. If you do not or cannot build a reliable vision then set interim goals and checkpoints and help people to work confidently and productively in a more ambiguous environment. A fuzzy vision is okay if the direction is always under active review and the organization and its people are comfortable with exploration and constant evolution.

If your organization doesn't have a vision or a strategy then develop one for your department that can be used to create an anchor for change. Take a look at the case study below which shows how one head of department addressed this problem in his organization.

CASE STUDY   Departmental vision

Pollards Construction had been led by two different CEOs over a five-year period. Neither of them had set a clear and sustainable direction for the company and this had led to a short-term, ad hoc view of investment. People within the organization had adopted a 'wait and see' approach as they watched project after project fail to get off the ground. Jim was appointed as the new head of internal operations. Learning about the history and sensing the inertia that had set in he worked with his team to create a vision and strategy for the internal operations department. Against this vision of success they reviewed current operations and conducted a transparent prioritization process. When they kicked off the first two improvement initiatives the teams hit the ground running as they already understood why the change was important and how it would contribute to the success of the department.

Directing the change

To build support for an ambitious change journey it must be clear where it is going and how that destination contributes to the overall success of the organization.

For those impacted by the change a clear direction helps them work out what the change means for them and whether they are willing to support it. For those delivering the change it provides the certainty they need to act confidently and the information to make the right decisions. For change leaders it provides a script for them to follow when talking about the change and rules for allocating valuable resources. A change vision is a multi-dimensional view of its success. Think of it as a movie showing the change working *in situ* – integrated with the organization, its customers and other initiatives. A good vision is easy to grasp, paints a desirable picture of the future and balances inspiration with a sense that it is achievable.

Why are we going there and why now?

When the vision for the change is clear, everyone involved will need to understand why that is the goal and why specific strategies have been chosen to get there. They'll need answers to the 'Why?' and 'Why now?' questions. If people are going to change the way they work they'll need a good reason. If you want them to build the right solution they'll need to know what problem they are trying to solve or opportunity they are trying to exploit. Change is primarily driven by either a proactive response to an opportunity or a reactive response to a danger in the form of a risk or a crisis. In the Coleridge Bank example the early vision to provide 'The Best Customer Service' was driven by an *opportunity* to get ahead of the competitors in the rankings. The second vision 'No. 3 for Mortgages' was driven by the *risk* of falling further behind in the market. The third vision 'Double our deposits' was driven by a *crisis* in funding availability.

Whilst most changes aimed at mitigating a risk will also provide opportunities for other improvements, an organization must agree the primary driver that has triggered the need for the change. For example, Solace and James, a law firm, intended to relocate one of its regional offices from the centre of the city to an area just north of the city. The people in that office were naturally concerned and wanted to know why this move was happening. Here's how the three managers in that office answered the 'why' and 'why now' questions when the move was announced.

Manager 1 – Margaret

Why? 'Because we need more space.'

Why now? 'Because our growth targets tell us we will run out of space by the end of the year.'

Manager 2 – Joe

Why? 'Because we want to provide you with better facilities.'

Why now? 'Because we think you've put up with sub-standard office accommodation for too long.'

Manager 3 – Chloe

Why? 'Because we need to reduce our real estate costs'

Why now? 'Because our lease is up for renewal at the end of this year.'

Whilst all these drivers may be true, it is easy to see how staff at that office can be confused by the mixed messages. Something as simple as this can create a significant wave of early resistance which is tough and time consuming to recover from. The leadership team must agree at the outset which primary driver they will communicate to bring about the change they need. Imagine how much more powerful it would have been to have heard the following response from all three managers.

Why? 'Because we need more space to meet next year's targets'

Why now? 'Because our lease is up for renewal at the end of this year and it has not been possible to negotiate the rent to a level we can afford.'

When everyone hears the same message it creates a solid starting point and makes it hard to doubt or challenge the reasons behind a change. This enables people to move on to the next stage of their exploration and find out more about it.

How will we get there?

Organizations that *direct* change have an easy to follow roadmap showing the improvements the organization wants to make, in what order and how

Figure 4.1.1   Integrated changes

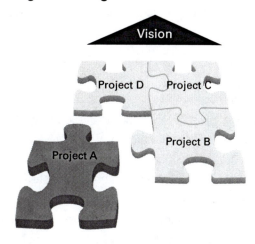

they all fit together (see Figure 4.1.1). The link to the organization's vision and strategy provides a clear understanding of how each change fits into the big picture.

> 32 per cent of companies performed redundant work because of un-harmonized projects (Meskendahl *et al*, 2011).

The change roadmap for the organization needs to be owned at the highest level and managed by an organization-wide change management office (CMO). The CEO and their direct reports must constantly reinforce the vision and the steps to achieving it. The strategy team are heavily involved but need to work more dynamically, collaboratively and transparently than in the past; seeing themselves as gatherers of important information and guides on the journey. Developing the initial roadmap can be a challenging task but the real value is in making sure it continues to provide accurate information to guide activities and decisions over time. The map must be kept up to date – with processes and forums in place to review and validate both the direction of the organization and the part that each change plays in that journey. Realignment along the way is normal and expected.

'A good strategy is one that is responsive to change' (Richard Rumelt).[16]

Once again, clear and consistent communication is critical if the roadmap is to provide effective direction to those on the journey. Many organizations believe the reporting from their strategy group or project management office (PMO) gives them the information they need. However, it is usually missing three critical elements. Firstly, the circulation is restricted to those who 'need to know' only. This is usually senior leaders or those involved in funding or managing major initiatives. Secondly, the information is not presented in a way that every employee can grasp easily or which enables them to understand the consequences for them. Thirdly, it is seen as static documentation which is rarely or secretly updated in response to changes in the environment. The case study below shows how one company developed their change roadmap.

CASE STUDY   Change roadmap

Pink Pig is a promotional products company providing a range of branded promotional items to the small to medium-sized business market. Over recent years they had remained competitive by scrambling to react to short-term threats. They had sourced lower-cost providers, updated the product range and made some tactical improvements to the website. The management team had not done any strategic planning for over three years and felt they were in survival mode. Their people were feeling ambushed by a range of conflicting priorities – first cost then product then technology. They felt the management team were not in control of the business.

The CEO met with the senior leadership team to discuss a longer-term approach and the need for a well-thought-through proactive strategy. Following a series of surveys, workshops and discussions with their teams, suppliers and customers they came together for two days to agree a direction for the organization and developed the roadmap shown in Figure 4.1.2.

Figure 4.1.2 Pink Pig integrated change roadmap

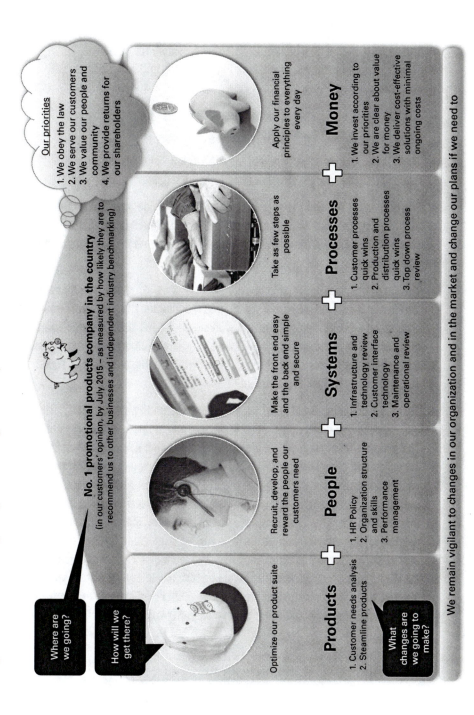

Let's look at how this plan helps their efforts to change.

- The picture is clear and easy to understand.

- The desired overall goal is clear – No.1 in the country for customer service. Everyone knows where Pink Pig is heading and how success will be measured.

- 'Our priorities' can remain static regardless of the strategy thereby providing some certainty to those making decisions.

- There is an acknowledgement that the road to the vision involves many side roads (products, people etc) that need to come together.

- The outcome from each stream is clear and can provide direction for the initiatives in that portfolio. For example, the IT department know that whatever changes they make it must 'make the front end easy and the back end simple and secure'.

- The list of changes or projects is clear and it is possible to see how these link through to the stream objective which in turn contributes to the overall goal of the organization. For example, someone working on the HR policy change can see that this is a key enabler for the 'people' strategic objective to 'Recruit, develop, and reward the people our customers need' which is one of the major routes required to realize Pink Pig's vision.

- There is a constant reminder in the statement that underpins the other components that plans can change in response to changes in the environment. The people working in Pink Pig are not surprised when some initiatives are cancelled and others are given a higher priority. This picture provides the context for explaining why these changes are made and what it means to the overall plan. For example, a few months after Pink Pig started using this roadmap they had the opportunity to purchase one of their competitors. This picture was used to explain why the competitor was a good strategic fit for the organization. In addition to a large customer base they had technology that would fast-track the IT strategic objective and there were opportunities to build a stronger product suite. They changed some of the projects listed in the plan to reflect merger activities while still using the overall framework with which staff were familiar.

Think ...

1 Does my organization have a clear direction and a roadmap to take us there?

_____

_____

_____

2 Why are we making this change?

_____

_____

_____

Why now?

_____

_____

_____

Direct traps

It makes perfect sense that people need to know where they are going and why before they will set out confidently on any change journey. So why don't we always provide the direction they need?

Trap 1: We don't know where we are going

Surprisingly many organizations operate without a clear vision of the required outcome. They invest in change initiatives that have no clear driver or benefit. Even when a business case is part of the process, developing and approving that case is still seen largely as a financial exercise. Whilst we may intend to realize non-financial benefits the mechanisms we use to give the 'go-ahead' for a change often don't provide answers to the basic questions about why we are doing it and what we need to get out of it – over and above a financial outcome. In this environment projects seem to spring up out of nowhere, often seeming to conflict with other initiatives. Without clear direction cynicism and inertia grow, projects flounder, people become demotivated and resources are wasted.

Trap 2: We are all going in different directions

We may all think we know where we are going but there is no guarantee that we are all thinking the same thing. Often direction is set following long periods of discussion, analysis and negotiation. During this time the senior leaders involved have each developed their own understanding of why the organization is embarking on a change. Is it any wonder that the team are confused when they hear three different answers to the question 'why are we changing?'

Trap 3: We know where we are going but we don't tell our people

Maybe we assume others don't need or want to know. Perhaps we think information about business strategy and change drivers is only relevant to senior leaders or that staff won't understand it. Perhaps we don't understand it! Sometimes we may feel that the direction is not clear enough to share and we are waiting until we have all the answers before we communicate. Perhaps we tell our internal staff but neglect to brief critical external stakeholders such as vendors and service providers. If their focus is different to ours we quickly feel the tension in the relationship.

Trap 4: We tell our people the direction but they don't understand

Whilst we may think we have told our people about the context and reasons for the change it often transpires that they have not understood it or have heard a different message to the one we thought we sent. This type of information is often provided at impressive town hall-style meetings where a senior leader announces the change to a large audience. Whilst this may give it the gravitas it deserves, it doesn't give the staff a chance to question, discuss and build their understanding of what they've been told. Often their managers are ill-equipped to answer questions after such sessions and confusion and scepticism quickly mount. Even when they do understand the information they often find it hard to see the relevance to the tasks they do every day. Whilst it may be relatively straightforward to communicate the drivers for your change (once you have agreed them!), communicating these in the context of each function is critical. If there is no attempt to check the message your audience have understood you won't know whether they are heading in the direction you need them to.

Trap 5: We don't reinforce the direction

When was the last time the project sponsor referred to your change in the context of the organization's strategy? Perhaps they haven't mentioned it since the original presentation, they rarely talk about it or when they do their references are vague. Do their decisions support the stated direction or do their actions seem to conflict with it? There can of course be a variety of reasons why this happens. Perhaps they don't see their peers doing it and are afraid to be the first advocate. Maybe they don't understand it, support it or feel a sense of ownership of it. The issue of ownership is common where external consultants are asked to develop a change vision and strategy on behalf of the leadership team thus inadvertently creating a feeling that the strategy is imposed. Whatever the cause, if we don't constantly reinforce the direction – with words *and* actions – it quickly fails to provide the focus we need to change.

Trap 6: The direction seems unachievable

Nothing drains the energy out of a team quicker than an unrealistic goal. If the majority of the people involved feel it can't be achieved they'll give up. As a leader it can be a difficult balance. We want to motivate people by setting an exciting new direction for the organization but if that vision is too different to the organization of today it is in danger of having completely the opposite effect to the one we need. Equally, if the suite of initiatives required to get us there seems more complex and challenging than anything we've done before we often ignore this despite our history of poor project delivery, disruptive change and inadequate benefit realization.

Trap 7: We expect the direction to remain the same

Change takes time to deliver sustainably and the environment in which our organization and our project operate doesn't stand still and wait for us to deliver. Change by its very nature means we are breaking new ground – doing things we haven't done before. Why then do we expect our initial direction to be 100 per cent right? Even if we are vigilant we may see that some of the drivers for our change have altered but in an attempt to retain certainty and control we bury our head in the sand and continue in the original direction. Some leaders think it shows weakness to change direction or cancel projects. For example, faced with new customer survey data which completely invalidated the drivers for a large change programme a senior executive was heard to say: 'A good leader stays true to their course no matter what'. In this situation quite the opposite was true. It was clear to everyone else in the organization that consumers were rapidly moving away from their core product and that a major change in direction was required if they were going to survive. Such leaders are often left gazing helplessly at data, plans and charts while their company quickly becomes irrelevant.

Trap 8: Our focus is only on short-term goals

A short-term perspective has crept into organizations and management thinking over recent years. CEO tenure is down to a global average of just over five years and this creates a short-term goal-driven view instead of a dynamic, longer-term vision approach.[17] A short tenure naturally makes CEOs reluctant to invest for future success. Shareholders seem to measure CEO performance by their ability to deliver tangible results regularly. This pressure on top of the uncertainty about the future can make CEOs reluctant to take the risks associated with transformational change. Setting a new course and sustainably aligning the organization and its people could take at least three years and the benefits in the first few years may be intangible. By contrast only four of the Harvard Business Review's Top 50 best performing CEO's in 2012 were in office for less than five years.[18] Short-term goals may motivate short-term initiatives but are often not seen as strong enough to anchor major change.

Trap 9: Our 'strategic planning' is actually 'financial planning'

In many of our organizations the real decisions about which changes to invest in are driven by financial processes and cycles and not business drivers, vision or strategy. We may even call our annual budgeting cycle 'strategic planning' but in reality it's got more to do with setting budgets than strategic investment. In some organizations departments are given an arbitrary figure to work to with but no visible link to the strategic priorities this must fund. Funding is set 6 months before the financial year and the annual nature of this cycle often means there is no mechanism to redirect resources with less than 18 months notice! Unfortunately our customers don't wait till next year's planning cycle to stop buying our product and our competitors don't wait politely in the wings before taking our market share!

Trap 10: We put blinkers on our change

We are clear about what we need to achieve and if only everyone else would get out of our way we'd be able to get there. We fail to recognize that our change is highly interdependent with a range of other activities and initiatives and that delivery of the organization's strategy is dependent on a harmonized programme of work of which we are only one cog in the wheel.

Think ...

1 Which of these traps is holding back your change?

2 Which one, if you fixed it, would bring the greatest benefit?

Direct tips

So now you've identified the things that are preventing you from setting a meaningful direction, what can you do to get off on the right foot?

Idea 1: Create a clear and compelling vision of your change

Change usually involves a combination of new processes, systems, mindsets and behaviours. Only when you show the integrated picture of these elements together will your people truly understand where the organization needs them to go. Whilst words on a page are a good start they are unlikely to provide the inspiration or confidence your people need to get on board quickly and remain focused. If you were trying to persuade them to come on a journey to the Antarctic you would show them colour pictures and maybe a film to give them a feel for what it would be like to be there. That's exactly what you need to do to provide a compelling and sustainable direction for your change. Develop the multi-dimensional full colour version of your vision. Use scenarios to show the players, their perspectives, the environment and the language being used. Show who is doing what and make sure the significant differences and benefits are illustrated. (See the questions at the end of this chapter for more help on how to do this.) This approach makes it easier for people to assimilate the information; it starts to answer their questions and builds a level of certainty and confidence. It also provides a memorable vision to guide their activities and decisions along the way.

Idea 2: Integrate your change into the organization's strategic roadmap

Develop and maintain an easy-to-understand roadmap of all the major changes in your organization, overlaid on business as usual activities. Critically it must show how each initiative fits with the others to deliver the vision for the organization. Keep the map up to date so that it reflects changes in the environment, the organization's vision and strategy. For example, if one initiative is de-scoped, delayed or cancelled how does this impact the rest of the map? New information can enable you to exploit additional opportunities to make your change journey easier, faster or more beneficial. Communicate updates by clearly explaining why and how the map has been realigned. As long as you articulate the rationale your staff will begin to see these dynamic realignments as a normal part of their work and agility as a key part of your competitive advantage.

Idea 3: Make it achievable

Are your stakeholders reluctant supporters because they don't believe the goal can be achieved? There may be great opportunities in the market but you need to be realistic about your ability to respond effectively to these. In the Coleridge Bank example it wasn't realistic to aim for 'No. 1 for Mortgages' so they aimed for 'No. 3'. If your performance is lagging behind or you are heavily focused on one product or market segment then changing to some-thing drastically different will require years of groundwork. If you don't have the luxury of years reset your sights on a vision more closely matched to your organization's current *culture, capacity, commitment* and *capability*.

Idea 4: Communicate the drivers and vision for your change

The initial communication of the drivers and vision is simple once you have the message and a choice of channels through which to send it. Starting with the *overall direction* of your organization, guide your audience through the roadmap to your change initiative – explaining where it fits into the big picture. Now move on to the *drivers for your change* – the answers to the 'why' and 'why now' questions. Explain the problem the organization needs to solve or the opportunity it wants to take. Then describe the *outcome the organization needs* – the vision of success and how it will be measured. The template in Appendix 6 will help you.

For example, if you were involved in the 'Customer Process Quick Wins' project at Pink Pig (see Figure 4.1.2) your message might look something like: 'In order for us to be (organization vision) the *No. 1 Promotional Products company in the country by July 2015* we need to make sure that (strategic objective) *we take as fewer steps as possible* in our processes. This project has been initiated because (drivers) *our customers have told us* that our ordering and payment processes feel longwinded. The outcome we need (change vision) is for *our customers to feel that dealing with us is quick, enjoyable and is an efficient use of their time.*'

Building on this initial message to achieve real understanding is where it can start to get complicated. For true commitment and focus your people need to internalize the direction. You'll need to identify the various audience groups who may be interested in or impacted by the change. Then understand the perspective of each of these groups and tailor your communication so it is relevant and meaningful for each of them. Zoom in on the relevant scenes and the characters of your vision so they can see how the change might impact them and their stakeholders. Use storytelling, scenarios and role plays to give them the full illustration of what their world will look like after the change. Open up a two-way communication process by providing opportunities for your stakeholders to question, discuss, role-play and expand on the vision.

Idea 5: Check for understanding

The larger and more diverse your audience, the greater the chance some of them will have taken away a different message to the one you thought you sent. Can everyone involved in or impacted by your change confidently and accurately articulate the drivers and vision for the change and how their role contributes to the overall success of the change and the organization? Don't assume they have interpreted the message in the right way. Check their interpretation and work hard to align their understanding before they head off in the wrong direction.

Idea 6: Talk consistently about your direction

Everyone involved in the change should always be ready to tell people quickly and succinctly why the change is happening, what outcomes the organization needs and where the change fits in the overall roadmap to the future. Provide the script of the 'right way' to talk about the change, its drivers, impact and outcomes. The template in Appendix 6 takes you through each of these questions to help you build a coherent story. Rehearse key leaders together until you are sure the message sounds consistent. It can still be authentic by using individual style and language but ensure the content of the message is the same – no matter who is delivering it.

Idea 7: Talk constantly about your direction

Repeat and reinforce the message at every opportunity. This change is supposed to be important to the organization's future so talk frequently, positively and knowledgeably about the drivers, scope and benefits. Perfect the elevator pitch and integrate it into communication at every opportunity. Many people are reluctant to keep repeating such a basic message but doing so has four big advantages. Firstly, your stakeholders are constantly reminded about and refocused on to where they are heading and why. Secondly, new employees or team members clearly understand the direction early in their tenure enabling them to get up to speed quickly. Thirdly, people who did not hear or fully understand the message the first time get another chance to catch up. Lastly, it provides a strong anchor for the change by building confidence that the drivers are real and important and that the vision is clear and consistent.

Idea 8: Reinforce the direction in actions as well as words

Talking about your direction is not enough; actions must reinforce the words. Every decision must reinforce the direction. A sceptical or nervous audience will be looking for anything that indicates that the direction is weak. Adapt or visibly stop activities that are not aligned to the stated direction. For example, if you want to build a more adaptive culture, change the annual performance cycle to one of ongoing performance review to demonstrate and support adaptability. Explain how the stated direction has influenced decisions. For example, if a solution is selected despite heavy opposition from staff, they will more readily get on board if you explain that it is the only solution available that supports the overall direction of the company.

Idea 9: Consider the direction as a constant work in progress

Having said the message needs to be clear and consistent the content of that message will change as new information comes to light from the project team, the organization and the outside environment. The change management office must act as a good *director* – in the 'crows nest' with a good view of both inside and outside of the organization. It is constantly picking up new information and relaying it to the 'captain' who then decides whether and how to change the course of the ship. If you need to change course explain why and help people to identify how their plans need to adapt as a result.

Idea 10: Direct confidently

Leading your people into the inevitable uncertainty of a new future is not for the fainthearted as we'll see in the next chapter. Consultation and involvement are important but your people also look to you for answers. If they are keen to make a contribution they need to know what contribution will be valued. They will get this information from your words and actions so send the right signals.

Think...

1 Which of these ideas could help your organization?

2 Which one would give you the most benefit?

So...

Before setting off on your change journey it is wise to make sure everyone knows where they are going, why and what they need to achieve.

1 What mechanisms are in place to enable the vision and strategy for both our organization and this change to be updated in the light of new information?

Organization vision and strategy:

_____

_____

_____

Change vision and strategy:

_____

_____

_____

2 What are the components of our vision 'movie'?

Scene 1: Perspective – a customer

Location:

_____

Characters:

_____

Change drivers to illustrate in this scene:

_____

_____

_____

Change benefits to illustrate in this scene:

_____

_____

_____

Important differences to highlight in this scene:

_____

_____

_____

Scene 2: Perspective – a staff member

Location:

_____

Characters:

_____

Change drivers to illustrate in this scene:

_____

_____

_____

Change benefits to illustrate in this scene:

_____

_____

_____

Important differences to highlight in this scene:

_____

_____

_____

Scene 3: Perspective – a shareholder, donor or taxpayer

Location:

_____

Characters:

_____

Change drivers to illustrate in this scene:

_____

_____

_____

Change benefits to illustrate in this scene:

_____

_____

_____

Important differences to highlight in this scene:

_____

_____

_____

Scene 4: Other stakeholder group (eg vendor, competitor or other)

Location:

_____

Characters:

_____

Change drivers to illustrate in this scene:

_____

_____

_____

Change benefits to illustrate in this scene:

_____

_____

_____

Important differences to highlight in this scene:

_____

_____

_____

3 How does our change initiative fit with other major initiatives in the organization to deliver its vision?

_____

_____

_____

4 If we asked our delivery team the following questions would they give broadly the same answers? *Why are we changing? Why are we changing now? What is changing? When is it changing? Who is impacted? What outcomes does the organization need?*

_____

_____

_____

5 If we asked each of our leaders the following questions would they give broadly the same answers? *Why are we changing? Why are we changing now? What is changing? When is it changing? Who is impacted? What outcomes does the organization need?*

_____

_____

_____

6 The most important thing I need to remember about *directing change* is...

_____

_____

_____

Want to know more?

Search engine terms: strategy, organization mission, organization vision, change vision, scenario planning, communicating strategy, communicating change.

Drive
the change

Drive: to cause and guide the movement of, take ownership, energize

Without the right drive you will not deliver the benefits your organization needs.

Figure 4.2   Drive the change

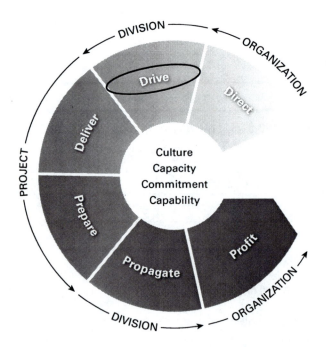

Successful organizations know how much energy it takes to change and *drive* their changes accordingly. They provide the change leadership to create sufficient momentum to guide the organization through the delivery of the change right up until the benefits are realized.

If *directing* change tells you where you are going then *driving* change provides fuel for the journey. *Drive* is the energy and momentum that keeps a change initiative moving forward. It is the energy that makes the change happen and prevents the old ways from settling back in. It calms negative perceptions whilst maintaining excitement and optimism about the future. Drive never loses sight of the end game. Energy levels will vary naturally during a long change journey and it is not appropriate to maintain high levels of energy over the period of months and years it takes to deliver most worthwhile changes. So the way in which the change is driven and the amount of energy provided needs to be adjusted along the way. There must be a balance between providing sufficient and appropriate *drive* to ensure progress continues whilst keeping enough in reserve to complete the journey.

> **Change is a marathon not a sprint.**

Most new initiatives start with a flurry of excitement and pizazz. Funding is allocated, projects launched and everyone is excited about being part of a new initiative. Over time the inevitable problems arise: shortage of resources, long timelines and delays; the project seems to 'run out of steam'. Once an initiative has lost its momentum it takes double the original effort to get it going again. More often than not it flounders until it either dies a natural death or someone puts it out of its misery!

The brakes can feel like they are on a change for a variety of reasons – most of them preventable. Figure 4.2.1 lists some of the events and circumstances that can contribute. Many of these, if they are allowed to continue, will result in visible tensions that will distract and potentially derail your change.

By contrast, there are many events that can provide the drive change needs. Figure 4.2.2 shows some examples of the events and circumstances that can act as a significant accelerator for change.

Figure 4.2.1   Causes of decreasing drive

⇩ Unclear reason for the change
⇩ Unclear vision of the future
⇩ Lack of support for decisions
⇩ Goal is perceived to be unachievable
⇩ Lack of belief in the value of the outcome
⇩ Ambiguity
⇩ Long timelines and delays
⇩ Lack of visible support from leaders
⇩ Unclear steps or timeline
⇩ Conflicts with organization's culture
⇩ Dissatisfied workforce

⇩ Multiple or conflicting priorities
⇩ Poor project publicity
⇩ Unclear roles and responsibilities
⇩ Inappropriate or inadequate resources
⇩ Inadequate knowledge skills and experience
⇩ Conflict within the project team
⇩ Conflict with vendors
⇩ Unforeseen obstacles and events
⇩ Change in direction
⇩ Periods of low project activity

Drive decreases with...

The driver

When the decision is taken to kick off a change initiative the driver needs to take the reins. Drive must come primarily from one senior leader who is usually assigned the role of sponsor or business owner. Whilst they will enlist the support of others they are accountable for ensuring progress is maintained and the benefits are delivered. The role of the *driver* is to stay focused on the outcomes, remove obstacles and provide energy to enable the team to maintain momentum right through to the delivery of benefits. The driver calms negative energy and builds and maintains positive energy. They set meaningful, consistent and achievable goals for people to commit to. They allow time, provide resources and encouragement and protect the delivery team from irrelevant demands. They manage the ups and downs along the way with a real belief that the people involved have the ability to overcome obstacles and remain on track. The driver must know where they are going and lead their people there – looking ahead, maintaining progress and motivating the team during the inevitable tough times.

Figure 4.2.2 Causes of increasing drive

Drive increases with...

⇧ Inspirational and consistent
  leadership
⇧ A good reputation for the project
⇧ A sense of making progress
⇧ Visible support from senior leaders
⇧ A clear direction and destination
⇧ Belief in the value of the outcome
⇧ A belief that the goal is achievable
⇧ Alignment to the organization's
  cultural forces
⇧ A few clear priorities
⇧ Contented workforce

⇧ Genuine support for decisions
⇧ A co-operative, collaborative and
  stimulating working environment
⇧ Clear steps and timeline
⇧ Clear roles and responsibilities
⇧ Appropriate and adequate
  resources
⇧ Adequate knowledge skills and
  experience
⇧ Transparent risk and issue
  management and decision making
⇧ Periods of high project activity

(Incidentally the majority of change leadership characteristics and activities outlined in this chapter are just as relevant to a line manager leading their team through a change as they are to your primary change leader.)

'When leaders make public their engagement in the difficult processes of change they become extraordinary teachers' (Robert Kegan and Lisa Lahey).[19]

Use the checklist below to see if your driver is fulfilling their role.

The role of the driver

✔ A driver **safeguards** the change on behalf of the organization
  by ensuring governance is in place, progress is being made,
  benefits will be delivered and resources are used judiciously.

✔ A driver **is an advocate** for the change. They build support by frequently referring to the change in a knowledgeable and positive way. They clearly articulate the facts and deal decisively with inaccurate or misleading information.

✔ A driver **brings the *direction* to life** so that everyone understands the need, the impacts, what's changing and the outcomes required. They tell stories and behave with a sense of urgency. If the destination and the impact are not yet clear they explain the steps that are being taken to gain more clarity.

✔ A driver **maintains** an appropriate level of **energy** throughout the change. When the energy is too high they calm concerned or overwhelmed stakeholders. When energy slumps to a level where progress is hampered they intervene to boost motivation and productivity. They know when to push the accelerator, when to ease off, when to change gear and when to apply the brake to the change so that everyone makes it to the finish line.

✔ A driver **balances project activity with business** priorities. They ensure the solution delivers the strategic intent whilst making sure it 'fits' the business sufficiently to be easily embedded. They keep a constant focus on both the solution development and the changes required in the business to be able to accommodate it. They constantly look out for changes in the environment which may necessitate a change in direction or approach.

✔ A driver maintains a **healthy and productive working environment** by creating and reinforcing a culture that rewards constructive behaviours and deals decisively with behaviours that will undermine success.

✔ A driver **removes obstacles** using their authority and other sources of power available to them.

✔ A driver **communicates** effectively to a wide range of people through a wide range of channels, constantly reiterating the need for the change and the benefits the organization needs.

✔ A driver enlists and **maintains** the **support of others** to expand their influence.

The right choice of driver is critical. It's a tough job and that person needs to remain effective, sometimes for years, until changes are truly embedded. When looking for the best person to perform this role start by looking for someone who has the following characteristics.

Situational characteristics of an effective change driver

- ✔ A genuine **belief in the value of the change**. The value may be to them personally, their business unit and/or the organization as a whole. This belief is likely to be strongest in someone who fully understands the change and has been involved in decisions about the scope and outcomes required.

- ✔ A **good 'fit'** for the change. You'll need someone who can role model the change and therefore has the right leadership style to suit. If the change is taking advantage of an opportunity the leadership can be more consultative or collaborative. If the company is in crisis you will need a strong leader who is willing to dictate direction. When your ship is sinking you don't want a choice of lifeboats; you just want to be told where to go!

- ✔ **'Skin in the game'**. To sustain the belief for the long haul look for someone who will feel personal consequences in relation to the change. This may be the threat of negative consequences for not delivering the benefits or a reward in the form of business performance, personal satisfaction or recognition. A reward aligned to their personal beliefs system will always provide more power for longer than motivation by coercion.

- ✔ **Authority**. The driver needs sufficient decision-making rights and these usually come with seniority. They must have access to the right resources, be able to make decisions and have sufficient authority to make change happen.

- ✔ **Business focus**. They must remain focused on the business outcomes of the change so are likely to be in a current business leadership role in the area that is impacted by the change.

- ✔ **A strategic thinker**. They need to be able to see connections, links and dependencies across a wide range of areas and activities inside and outside the organization.

✔ **Stable**. The role of driver is a long-term one so it is important to select someone who is expected to stay in the role for the foreseeable future.

✔ **Capacity**. Look for someone who has or can create the time required to dedicate to this role in addition to their other responsibilities. Driving requires concentration.

✔ **Experience**. A team will not be easily inspired by someone who has less experience than they do. At the very least the driver will need to have some experience of projects and how they work. If they have experience of a similar change or challenge they will be seen as a more credible messenger and will gain support more quickly.

For some changes, it may not be clear who the *driver* should be. The case study below shows how one organization resolved this issue.

CASE STUDY   Who should drive?

Back at Coleridge Bank, there was disagreement about who should sponsor a regulatory change programme – the retail bank division or the compliance department? To settle the issue they asked themselves two questions. Firstly, '*Who has the most to lose if the changes don't stick?*' This highlighted the fact that although it is the compliance department's job to make sure the business is compliant, it is the retail bank division that has the most to lose if they are found not to be. They would pay the fines and suffer the brunt of the brand damage. Secondly, they asked '*Where do we need to make the most changes to our people, processes and systems?*' It was clear that the processes and systems that needed to change in order to become compliant were also in the retail bank division and these people would need their leaders to be strong advocates for the change if it was going to stick. It was therefore agreed that effective sponsorship would come from the retail bank division and not the compliance department.

> ### Finding the right sponsor
>
> *'Who has the most to lose if the changes don't stick?'*
> *'Where do we need to make the most changes to our people, processes and systems?'*

Another area where identifying the right driver can seem difficult is for a change which will impact the whole organization. Given that most organizations operate in silos of clearly delineated departments or sub-organizations, and the driver needs to be able to motivate and influence everyone involved, the role naturally falls to the executive who sits at the pinnacle of the impacted business units – usually the CEO. For changes with a far-reaching impact the driver will need to be supported by active and visible change leaders within each of the business units but the driver role cannot be delegated and expected to be as powerful.

Driving skills and attributes

> 'Lead like a relentless but reflective bulldoze driver... demanding, patient and persistent' (Faull and Fleming, 2005).

A good change *driver* is ready, willing and able to drive the change effectively over a long period. In his book, *A Sense of Urgency* (2008), John Kotter says that a change leader must be 'visible, determined, self-confident, non-blaming, passionate and competent'. So when the shortlist of people with the situational characteristics has been drawn up you can refine the list even further by considering the critical personal characteristics required to make your driver a success. The best change driver will usually be one of the most popular and effective leaders in the organization and will already have demonstrated the following attributes:

✔ A good driver is influential. They are trusted and respected by those around them; they create visions and inspire people towards them. The driver needs to motivate people to do things they've never done, take risks and to go places they've never been. They must have, or be able to quickly build, the trust and respect of a wide range of stakeholders at all levels both inside and outside the organization.

✔ A good driver is a role model. They consistently demonstrate the behaviours the organization needs to be successful and are calm in the face of problems and unexpected events. If the change needs a shift in mindset the driver will already demonstrate that new mindset.

✔ A good driver is confident and brave. The change driver leads from the front and must not be afraid to set out the path. Consultation and involvement of those impacted is clearly important for change success but leaders who value this collaborative approach are often reluctant to provide strong direction when the change necessitates it.

✔ A good driver is an excellent communicator. They use simple language, avoid jargon, listen and check for understanding. They are skilled in the use of storytelling to communicate context and vision. They understand the need to consult, keep people informed, and give clear direction. They are clear about what is and isn't changing and are not afraid to admit they don't have all the answers.

✔ A good driver is a principled negotiator. They ensure they have all the information and genuinely collaborate to obtain the best outcome for the change, the organization and all those involved.

✔ A good driver is seen as a fair leader. They communicate the rationale for decisions, reward constructive behaviours and deal decisively with behaviours that will undermine success.

✔ A good driver is able to empower people. They demonstrate belief in their capability, provide opportunities to learn and make the right resources available.

✔ A good driver is open. They listen to and actively consider new information, ideas and conflicting views and use this to inform a change in their views when appropriate.

✔ A good driver is realistic. They set motivating but achievable goals and acknowledge challenges and obstacles along the way.

A good driver acknowledges difficulties but makes it clear those difficulties aren't going to prevent ultimate success.

The best drivers have a range of critical personal attributes that underpin these observations. Firstly, they are self-aware and have a good understanding of their strengths and limitations. They are highly skilled at identifying and managing their emotions and those of others. They have a high tolerance for ambiguity and a low need for control. The driver is a very visible role and the necessary exposure will not suit everyone. They must confidently take up the driver's seat from the outset but being the first to demonstrate support for a change can be a terrifying leap of faith. Major change poses a significant personal risk for those who play the role of driver: there is high potential for failure. Great change drivers are persistent and resilient. They understand that change is a marathon not a sprint.

CASE STUDY Michael was the best driver we'd ever had...

Michael was a general manager at an insurance company. He had been asked to be the sponsor for a programme which aimed to transform the back office functions he managed to be more aligned to the needs of the customer. Over the years, the teams had become focused on their technical function and their processes and systems made it hard to respond quickly to customer needs.

Michael really believed in this transformation. He could see clearly how this change fitted into the direction the company wanted to take and had been involved in all the decisions. In his previous company he had managed the customer service area and had a strong belief in aligning operations to customer needs. Over the next year Michael worked hard to change people's perspectives, processes and systems. Whenever Michael was chatting to staff or his colleagues on the executive, he would never fail to mention the work of the programme, how important it was for the organization, the achievements and progress it was making. In the lunch queue, in every staff address, in meetings... even in the bathroom!! He made no apologies for his enthusiasm and everyone he came into contact with knew what was important.

Michael understood that he couldn't be the only person driving the change and coached his team leaders in the skills and activities of a good change leader until the change was being driven by a united band of committed leaders.

As the transformation progressed, he, the project manager and the change manager worked closely together. When the project manager faced an obstacle they couldn't deal with, Michael would step in to clear the way. When the project team became dispirited he would go and talk to them to about why the project was still critically important to the organization and its customers. He soon gained a reputation for letting nothing stand in their way.

After 18 months Michael was offered a promotion to the sales director position. This was a great move for him and he accepted it. Before he moved across he was asked to recommend a replacement for his operations role. As well as finding someone with the right skills and experience he looked for someone who would continue the passion and energy for the transformation – someone who really cared about improving the customer's experience. Jennifer fitted the bill and Michael spent many hours behind the scenes sharing information, coaching her in the competencies required, integrating her into the programme and getting her up to speed before officially handing over the reins.

Think...

1   The last time I saw a significant spike in energy in our change project it

    was positive/negative_____ and was caused by _____

    _____

    _____

    _____

2   The last time I saw a significant slump in energy in our change project it

    was positive/negative_____ and was caused by _____

    _____

    _____

    _____

Drive traps

So it's easy to see how being able to maintain momentum is critical for effective change. Without sufficient drive progress will be slow, it becomes difficult to overcome the inevitable challenges and the potential for failure increases significantly. So let's look at why your change may not have the fuel it needs to complete the journey.

Trap 1: Our projects take too long to deliver anything tangible

Not only is this bad for your return on investment it's an energy-sapping long journey for the delivery team with little sense of progress or achievement to keep them motivated. The people in the business learn to ignore or become sceptical about the change as it seems like it is 'all talk'.

Trap 2: We ignore the warning signs

We know the relationship with the vendor is not as collaborative as we'd like, we're aware there are some tensions within the project team, we know there is an unavoidable quiet spot in the project timeline but we don't put anything in place to manage the effect these events will have on the momentum and progress of the project. Sometimes we don't anticipate the damage these events can do and sometimes we just hope they will go away without us having to tackle them.

Trap 3: Our culture saps the energy from our change

If antagonism or scepticism are a strong part of 'the way we do things around here' the driver will have their work cut out. If the cultural forces at play do not support the change or your driver they will constantly feel like they are pushing it uphill.

Trap 4: We underestimate the role of the driver

The person identified as the sponsor can often have purely financial or governance duties. They chair project steering committee meetings and sign off documents but we don't ask them to perform any visible leadership role. If they are held responsible for anything it is the delivery of the project and not the delivery of the benefits. In some projects the role of sponsor appears to be purely ceremonial with no practical value to the programme whatsoever!

Trap 5: Our driver doesn't understand the role

Our project management methodology tells us we must appoint a sponsor and we duly appoint a suitable individual. For some reason we expect them to understand what is required of them and so often this is not the case. Many ineffective sponsors just don't know what they should be doing. They take a passive approach, waiting for the project manager to tell them what they need. They aren't driving – they are being a passenger. Without realizing it they are pushing the project manager into the driving seat and with the best will in the world your project manager is not able to drive *and* deliver the change convincingly.

Trap 6: We assume our driver knows how to drive

As we've seen, being a good driver takes a rare combination of skills, knowledge and experience, not to mention personal attributes. Significant change doesn't happen very often and it's entirely possible that your sponsor has either never done the job before or is a novice. For some reason we assume that, as they are a senior leader, they must have what it takes to be a great change leader.

Trap 7: Our driver is not a convincing advocate

'No individual lemming ever got bad press' Charles Roxburgh (2003).

Actions speak louder than words and there is no situation that highlights this more than a change leader who doesn't really understand or believe in the change. Being a good driver is the hardest role in any change. Often the decisions have been made by others and the driver is given accountability for making it happen. Within a short period of time they are expected to get up to speed on the details of the change, work out what it means to them personally and to their team. They have to develop a clear and compelling vision and a way of communicating this consistently. Then they need to put their head above the parapet and be the first person in their organization to visibly support the change. This takes enormous personal courage, resilience and energy and unless the driver has worked through the things that are getting in the way of them being an authentic champion it will be clear to everyone around them that they don't believe what they are saying. If the leader doesn't intend to change they won't either.

The 'Emperor's New (change) Clothes'

You may remember the story of the proud Emperor who didn't want to appear stupid in front of his tailors. They pretended to design a fabulous suit of clothes for him, told him how wonderful he looked and sent him out to parade in front of his people naked. Organizational change is unlikely to send you out physically naked in front of your people but for those without a robust self-esteem it is not unusual for them to pretend they understand. They go along with the tide of opinion in order to fit in and not appear stupid or a 'trouble-maker'. Despite being told 'there is no such thing as a silly question' it is surprising how many leaders do not really understand the changes they are being asked to support but are too worried about what others will think to ask questions. When briefed on the change they nod and give the answers that person wants to hear. Their lack of real understanding then prevents them from contributing the level of energy required to fulfil the role they need to.

Trap 8: Our drivers often drive whilst distracted

Many changes run out of steam or lose their way because the driver does not have the time to fulfil the role. They delegate their driving responsibilities to other people with less power and influence. Inertia and wheel-spinning quickly set in when the driver takes their foot off the pedal. Our projects still appear to be busy but they are not making any meaningful progress.

Trap 9: We assign a sponsor with no 'skin in the game'

Often we'll mistakenly look for a driver within the department that has the subject matter expertise to deliver a change. However, unless they will feel the pain of failure they are not the right choice for a driver. The risk team won't be the ones going to prison if the new regulatory changes don't stick. The IT department will still get paid even if the new system doesn't deliver its benefits.

Trap 10: We assign multiple drivers

We assign equal decision-making authority and accountability for outcomes across all our sponsors. This is often deemed necessary so that the workload is shared or because the change impacts on multiple business units. Whilst this may well be the case, imagine how slowly your car would go if you had three people driving it! If we have an overconsultative culture or our leaders shy away from accountability we are much more likely to spread this role over several people often sending mixed messages about our direction, creating gaps in the leadership and slowing the change down.

Think...

1 Which of these traps is holding back your change?

2 Which one, if you fixed it, would bring the greatest benefit?

Drive ideas

So when you've removed a few of the brakes from your change there are plenty of things you can do to provide the drive you'll need.

Idea 1: Set yourself up for success

A new change initiative naturally has energy when it is launched and it is important to leverage this whilst it is available so before you embark on your change journey do some checks. Make sure your driver is in place and is ready, willing and able to welcome everyone to the change and get them up and running quickly with clear direction and authentic advocacy. If your driver is absent or still learning to drive when you kick off your change understand that this will impact on your ability to get off to a strong start.

Idea 2: Plan ahead

From the moment you decide to embark on a change there are several things you already know will either energize or sap the energy from the journey. If you are embarking on a road journey and you know that there are roadworks ahead you can either continue to drive down the road until you see them or you can plan to take a different route to avoid the delays. If you know there are elements of your culture, processes or previous projects that usually help or hinder change identify what these are and how you will leverage or avoid them. Look for clues in your project plan. Where are the natural peaks and troughs in activity and therefore energy? The period before major milestones is usually a high-energy time as everyone strives to meet the deadline. How will you regulate the inevitable stress that comes with this time and maintain focus and quality? By contrast there may be low-energy periods whilst the team wait for the results of a consultation exercise. Look at the plan from the perspective of the people impacted: maybe they will be invited to the launch but when will the next big news item be available for them? How will your approach accommodate the busy or quiet periods in a way that maintains sufficient and appropriate momentum?

Idea 3: Deliver change in smaller chunks

It is easier to motivate people to complete short journeys than long ones so 'chunk' your change so that the team can focus on a shorter deadline. Many organizations now split their changes into a series of shorter projects. Consider a prototype approach – developing and refining the change *in situ*. Not only does this provide greater motivation for teams and faster delivery of changes it reduces risk through meaningful involvement of change recipients and provides a more agile base from which to change direction when needed.

Idea 4: Be alert and act quickly on warning signs

It can be tempting to ignore the warning signs in the hope they will fix themselves. A good driver remains open to information from inside and outside of the organization. When they sense the change is beginning to have more or less energy than is good for it an effective driver will immediately assess the cause, work out if or how it will impact on the overall journey and, when necessary, take action to calm or energize as appropriate. If they discover the change is no longer needed or the outcome is no longer appropriate a good driver will act swiftly to stop or redirect the journey. This needs the courage and humility to stop or redirect projects that may already have soaked up considerable time, energy and resources. If the driver has been publically championing the change they now need to go back out and explain why something that was so dear to them last week is no longer seen as important. This can be a very humbling experience.

Idea 5: Spread the influence

One leader is not able to provide all the fuel required to drive your change. It's impossible for them to have their eyes and ears across every stakeholder group let alone influence them all effectively. So a good driver will recruit both formal and informal leaders to help them. John Kotter calls this a 'guiding coalition'; a group of influential people who can influence and monitor views and activities in their area and either fix problems or refer them to the driver. These people are seen as local ambassadors for the change. In the early stages whilst resources are being made available and commitment is building these people are more likely to be formal leaders in senior positions. In the later stages of a change this role is more likely to be played by line managers and informal leaders – people within the organization who influence others. A good driver will also find other ways of reinforcing the momentum by adapting processes, systems and the physical environment to align to and reinforce the new way of working.

Idea 6: Communicate

Just about every piece of research on the reasons change fails has two common elements in the top three causes – lack of visible leadership and poor communication. It's easy to see why, if you can't see who is leading the change and you are not getting the information you need, your commitment levels are going to be very low. The driver's role is 'front and centre' – continually visible and accessible – always advocating for the change. So what does the driver need to communicate continually to maintain focus and momentum?

> **Facts**. Organizational change creates a great deal of uncertainty which our brains are hardwired to see as a threat and as a natural response we fill the gaps with our own assumptions and interpretations. The driver must always clearly articulate the facts about what they know and importantly what they don't yet know about the change.

> **Why are we changing and why now?** If the drivers for the change aren't clear then everyone involved will be looking back over their shoulder throughout the journey. Whilst they may eventually agree to comply with the change, compliance will always be underpinned with a level of energy-sapping doubt or resentment if the trigger for the change is not clear.

A compelling vision of the outcome. The driver needs to communicate such a compelling vision that those following will find it irresistible.

Make progress visible. The people impacted by the change may have ignored it for a while and the team delivering it are often too close to the detail to realize the progress they are making. It is the driver's job to highlight where they are at in the journey and how far they've come.

Build belief in achievability of goals. Change is full of seemingly unachievable goals – things people haven't done before. The driver needs to clearly demonstrate that they believe the vision is achievable as well as desirable and that they believe the team have what it takes to get there. A good driver acknowledges difficulties but makes it clear those difficulties aren't going to prevent ultimate success.

Make decisions transparent. An important part of building and maintaining trust is explaining what decisions are being made, who is making them and how the outcomes were reached. Even if people don't agree with the decision, they are more willing to go along with it if the rationale is clear.

Idea 7: Pick the right driver

Your change simply won't get the momentum it needs if your driver doesn't have the power to remove obstacles, provide resources and make decisions. They won't have the effect you need unless they can cause a wide range of people to change their beliefs. Remember to look for the right leadership style to suit your change – do you need someone who is consultative or directive? How fast do you need to implement the change and how much resistance are you expecting? Bearing in mind the *role* they must play look for the situational *characteristics* you'll need then make sure they have the personal *attributes* required to be effective for the long haul. Use the template in Appendix 7 to help you.

Idea 8: Give driving lessons

Many senior managers appointed to project sponsor roles do not understand what they need to do. The subtleties and priorities of the role will be different for every change so expect to clearly articulate the role you need your driver to play at each stage of the change – right down to the behaviours the change needs them to demonstrate and the outcomes they need to achieve. You should also expect to fill some gaps in their knowledge or capability before they can confidently play the role you need them to play.

CASE STUDY   Learning to drive

Jo, the head of customer services at a telecommunications company, had been asked to lead a large transformation programme. The changes would impact on nearly everyone in her department as well as her customers. She was seen as a confident and decisive leader who was popular with her team. In the three years she had been in the role she had turned around the culture within the department and was getting some impressive business results. Despite being an experienced executive she had never led a large change project. Whilst she was flattered to be asked, she realized that she didn't fully understand what the role entailed nor was she confident that she had what it would take to do it well.

Before the change got under way she worked closely with the change manager and the project manager to agree the scope of the role and the outcomes she needed to achieve. She then worked with the human resources department to conduct a 360-degree feedback assessment that helped her to identify some of her gaps and blind spots. She quickly put together a development plan that would provide the support she needed to build the knowledge and skills to effectively drive the change.

Idea 9: Hold the driver accountable

The best way to ensure that your driver maintains their own momentum is to ensure there are real consequences for them if the change does not deliver the benefits. To reinforce the focus throughout the change journey the driver needs to feel real reward for demonstrating the right behaviours and making good progress and real pain for a delay to benefits realization or allowing benefits to be unduly compromised. However you do it you need to keep your driver focused and productive right through until the benefits are realized. The example below shows how a threat of consequences can still sometimes fail to motivate a driver if it is not handled well.

CASE STUDY   Accountability can fail to motivate

Tom was head of manufacturing at a small white goods company. A project had been initiated by the finance department to cut the waste out of the processes in his area and he had been appointed as sponsor. As Tom started to get to grips with the change he discovered that the business case had been signed off and had estimated savings of $2 million which had already cut from his following year's budget. Tom and his team had not input to the business case and he could not understand where the figure had come from. It looked like the project team estimates had not taken into account the existing operation or the other initiatives going on is his area. Without a clear understanding of how the $2 million was to be saved it was almost impossible for Tom to confidently and authentically support the change. As the money had already been taken out of his budget for the following year he felt under extreme pressure to deliver the project on time otherwise he would have to make the sacrifice without the changes and this would mean cuts elsewhere in his business. He was clearly a reluctant driver with wavering support for his own change.

Idea 10: Provide ongoing support for your drivers

Whether it's your sponsor or any other change leader, driving change can be a lonely job. It is a risky endeavour that requires real guts. A driver is often the messenger of controversial information. They make decisions that are not always popular and they allow themselves a significant level of personal exposure when they are the visible face of a change. They must sustain their own energy while creating conditions for others to restore theirs. All of this takes a toll and in their quiet moments most drivers question whether they are tough enough to keep it up. They therefore need a lot of support, particularly from peers and their manager, and must be rewarded for engaging proactively and visibly with the risks. Their position as driver and their messages must be visibly and frequently respected, supported and reinforced by others. They must have easy access to a range of personal and professional support mechanisms including people from inside and outside of the organization such as their manager, organizational change experts, human resources professionals, counsellors and coaches.

Think...

1 Which of these ideas could help your organization?

2 Which one would give you the most benefit?

So...

Before setting off on your change journey it is wise to plan ahead to avoid obstacles and make sure you have a driver who is going to take you all the way. The change driver assessment in Appendix 7 will help you identify and evaluate your change driver but in the meantime the following questions will give you some insights into what you are facing.

1 What activities, events, processes, systems or people do we think will sap the energy from our change journey?

_____

_____

_____

_____

What can we do to prevent or minimize the impact?

_____

_____

_____

_____

2 What activities, events, processes, systems or people do we think will trigger negative energy that will distract people from the goal?

_____

_____

_____

_____

What can we do to prevent or manage the impact?

_____

_____

_____

_____

3 Which time periods will have low levels of visible activity or progress from the perspective of someone in the *delivery* team?

_____

_____

_____

_____

What can we do to regulate momentum during these periods?

_____

_____

_____

_____

4 Which time periods will have low levels of visible activity or progress from the perspective of those in the *impacted* team?

_____

_____

_____

_____

What can we do to regulate momentum during these periods?

_____

_____

_____

_____

5 What can we do to improve the effectiveness of our driver?

_____

_____

_____

_____

6 The most important thing I need to remember about _driving_ change is ...

_____

_____

_____

_____

Want to know more?

Search engine terms: leadership, change leadership, inspirational leadership, followers, self-management, self-awareness, resilience, advocacy, emotional intelligence, coaching.

Deliver the change

Deliver: to carry and turn over (goods, etc) to the intended recipient or recipients

Without the right delivery people, systems and processes you will not achieve the benefits your organization needs.

Figure 4.3 Deliver the change

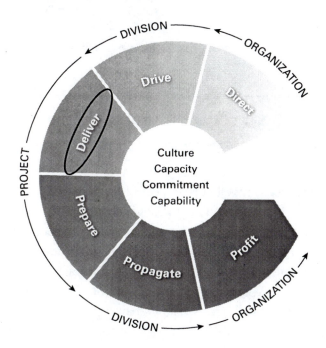

Deliver is the home of the traditional project. Successful organizations start with a clear need (*direction*) and an active customer (*driver*) and reliably deliver appropriate solutions. Delivery takes an idea from a concept, through selecting and designing the best solution, testing it, implementing it and handing it over to the people who will look after it. Success is largely measured by the ability to deliver the right solution, on time and budget.

Delivery relies on good project management and this is where most organizations start their journey of change maturity. Typically ad hoc initiatives owned by line managers become dedicated projects with their own budgets, resources and reporting. Someone is assigned as the project manager and over time project management becomes recognized as an important strategic organizational capability. Much has been written about project management so this chapter will not teach you how to manage a project. What it will do is to put project management and the project lifecycle in the context of organizational change and explain what you should and should not expect from your projects.

Organizations that see change as an 'add-on' to their business often think that a project is all it takes to change the organization. They assume the project team will take care of the change and everyone else can get on with their job until it's time to implement it. They leave all aspects of the change to the project team – including decisions for which they have no experience, authority or responsibility. When the change is implemented what's left of the project team move on to their new jobs a week or two after implementation.

Change is bigger than projects.

Successful organizations know that change involves more than just a project and that the project is only one part of the entire change process. They see change as a natural part of their business and know that project activity must be integrated into a wider set of business decisions, activities and priorities. They consider the project management cycle as a subset of the change lifecycle and project delivery to be just one of several enablers of business benefits. This is one of the biggest shifts in thinking an organization goes through before it can reliably deliver the benefits it needs. Figure 4.3.1 below shows where the *delivery* of the change fits in the overall series of activities required to successfully change an organization.

Figure 4.3.1 Relationship between the change and project lifecycles

CHANGE LIFECYCLE

DIRECT   DRIVE   DELIVER   PREPARE   PROPAGATE   PROFIT

PROJECT LIFECYCLE
Concept   Scoping   Execution   Closure

In the early stages of change maturity an organization may assume the change lifecycle is a subset of the project lifecycle and that change only happens during the implementation period. As maturity increases they begin to see the project lifecycle as the same as the change lifecycle with the appointment of the project team being the start of the change and the end of the project symbolizing the end of the change.

Figure 4.3.1 shows how successful *delivery* is dependent on a clear *direction* and the energy of a good *driver* to provide the momentum it needs. In the weeks and months before our project was officially launched many people were engaged and important decisions were made. These were all critical activities in the laying of the foundations – understanding who made what decisions, when, using what information and assumptions; who liked it, who didn't and what risks were identified. When the project is up and running *delivering* the change is not the only focus with a need to pay as much attention to *preparing* for change during this time. When the change is implemented success is dependent on areas outside of the control of the delivery team such as the willingness and ability of impacted line managers to *propagate* the change and the availability of mechanisms that enable the business to know whether they are *profiting* from it.

Project programme and portfolio management

The building of project management maturity is often the precursor to organizational change maturity. Many organizations start with little or no formal project delivery structures, processes or language. As the risk level of their projects increases they typically bring in specialist project management skills and formal processes to standardize and control project delivery. They develop or adopt a project management methodology and tools to enable them to consistently guide and govern progress. Successful organizations continually review their project management processes, methods and structures to ensure they support business strategies and remain focused on business outcomes.

As the size and complexity of the changes increase organizations move to managing 'programmes' of work which bring together several related projects

Figure 4.3.2 Pink Pig delivery governance structure

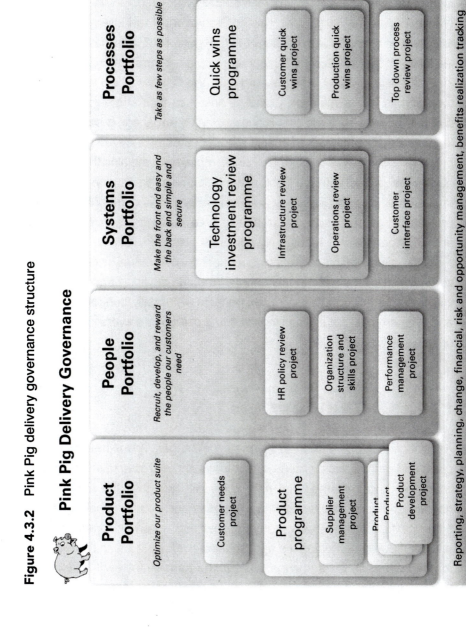

Pink Pig Delivery Governance

Product Portfolio	People Portfolio	Systems Portfolio	Processes Portfolio
Optimize our product suite	*Recruit, develop, and reward the people our customers need*	*Make the front end easy and the back end simple and secure*	*Take as few steps as possible*

Product Portfolio

Customer needs project

Product programme

Supplier management project

Product ...

Product development project

People Portfolio

HR policy review project

Organization structure and skills project

Performance management project

Systems Portfolio

Technology investment review programme

Infrastructure review project

Operations review project

Customer interface project

Processes Portfolio

Quick wins programme

Customer quick wins project

Production quick wins project

Top down process review project

Reporting, strategy, planning, change, financial, risk and opportunity management, benefits realization tracking

We apply our financial principles to everything every day

under one umbrella. Organizations that need to reliably deliver a multitude of complex changes will introduce 'portfolios' of projects and programmes aimed at delivering a chunk of the organization's strategy. Within each portfolio resources can be allocated and priorities changed to suit the ever-shifting landscape without losing sight of the overall strategic objective.

In an earlier chapter we met Pink Pig Promotional Products and their clear roadmap of change for the organization. Figure 4.3.2 shows how they use the three levels of delivery management to plan, control and reliably deliver their projects. It shows how they organize the delivery of the various initiatives across four investment portfolios linked to their strategic direction – product, people, systems and processes. Where managing some projects together as one entity would enable a better outcome they are grouped into programmes within each portfolio. For example, by combining the 'Customer quick wins' project with the 'Production quick wins' project the programme manager is able to use common skills, methods and reporting for both projects. They are also able to identify and manage any overlaps whilst allowing each team to focus on the different perspectives.

As the principles are the same no matter how the delivery is organized the term project will be used in this chapter to mean anything from an informal initiative right through to a complex portfolio of formally controlled projects and programmes. Let's take a look at some of the key players in the delivery of your change.

Project manager

A critical role in any delivery is the project manager. This is the person who plans and orchestrates a range of resources and activities to select, design, build, test and implement the right solution. They have the ability to sort activities, roles and resources into a cohesive and comprehensive plan and then use that plan to track, communicate and report on progress. Their primary focus is on getting the right solution across the line in the least time for the least cost. If the change is managed formally they will have access to a suitable project management methodology and have the skills to apply it appropriately. A good project manager is also competent in areas such as financial and risk management.

This role is typically the domain of people who prefer to work in a structured way and are comfortable using their authority as well as other indirect sources of power to maintain progress. A good project manager can bring order out of chaos, is a structured thinker and a clear communicator. They are determined, resilient and persistent but are flexible enough to allow for new information and demonstrate a constructive approach to the inevitable obstacles along the way. A good project manager combines these attributes with an ability to build and maintain effective stakeholder relationships whilst being a great people leader and role model to their team.

The project manager is not the owner or leader of the change. They own the development and delivery of the solution and they are the leader of the project team but they will often move on once that solution is delivered.

Project team

Assuming the change is big enough to warrant a team to deliver it the range of people who make up the project team will vary enormously depending on the type of change and its stage of evolution. Aside from the relevant subject matter expertise these people will thrive and be productive if they are suited to a project environment. High-performing delivery team members are motivated by working as part of a team to see an idea come to life. They are likely to take pride in the part they play in designing, building or testing the solution. In the early stages of the change project team members must be good at conceptual thinking and comfortable working collaboratively in an ambiguous environment. As the design of the change becomes clearer the emphasis shifts to a focused and diligent approach to building and testing the solution and affecting a smooth handover. For this you'll need people who can plan and organize their own work, have an eye for detail, manage risks, overcome obstacles and meet deadlines.

Some of your project team may come from the business area that will be impacted by the change. Whilst co-opting business representatives onto project teams is a great way of ensuring alignment with the business it must be done with care. The case study below tells the story of Sarah from the sales team of an IT services company. She was brought into the project team that was managing the introduction of a new IT equipment monitoring service that would be offered to customers.

CASE STUDY   Involving business representatives in the delivery team

Sarah had been working in the sales team of BTS, an IT services company, for three years. Prior to that she had worked in the CEO's office for two years which had given her great insight into how the different departments within the organization worked. She had a good relationship with the heads of department and an in-depth knowledge of what clients needed. When BTS kicked off a project to build a new IT equipment monitoring service Sarah seemed like the ideal person to recruit onto the team. She would be able to help the team remain focused on the customer needs and provide essential knowledge about how the service would be operationalized, marketed and used.

Sarah had been spending the majority of her time with clients so her car had been her desk. The move to the project team meant she would be spending all her time in the office with the rest of the delivery team and she was not sure how she would feel about this. She was keen to take up the opportunity to work on such an exciting project though so was confident she could adjust.

As the design phase progressed Sarah began to feel more and more out of her depth. Everyone around her seemed to speak a different language – 'phase' 'stage-gate' 'deliverable' 'milestone' 'Gantt' 'project initiation document' 'risk log'. She didn't know what any of it meant and there didn't seem to be anyone willing to explain.

When she attended meetings it was hard for her to get her point across among the myriad of experts. They all seemed to have strong views about what they thought the service should look like even though none of them had ever spoken to a client or knew anything about the way the organization operated! The rest of the project team barely noticed that Sarah had become increasingly silent during these discussions and no one seemed to be aware of the risk that there was very little business or customer input going into the design of the service.

Sarah was also dealing with an unexpected change in the way her work was managed. She was used to a flexible way of working where she had considerable autonomy. Working in the project meant working as part of a team and having to meet deadlines that seemed to be somewhat out of her control. She wasn't used to planning her activities ahead of time and being held to a timeline and approach. She started to miss deadlines and the project manager became increasingly frustrated by what he saw as her inability to deliver.

Sarah's old boss, Angela the head of sales, saw Sarah in the car park one morning and couldn't help noticing that she was not her usual sparkling self. Sarah shared with her the difficulties she was having adjusting to the project team environment. Angela could see how upset and frustrated Sarah was and suggested they go for a coffee. Not long after they sat down Angela pulled out a napkin and took a pen from her bag. 'Tell me how it should work when someone from the business has a valuable role to play in a project,' she said... Over the next 20 minutes they drafted the following guidelines in Figure 4.3.3...

Figure 4.3.3   Guidelines for involving business people in projects

1. Constantly demonstrate a belief that the views and priorities of customers and people impacted by the change are critical to success

2. Before appointing business representatives to the project team make them aware of the working environment, how their success will be measured and what help is available to support their transition

3. Induct business representatives into the project by explaining project expectations, language and roles

4. Ensure the effective use of business knowledge and expertise in all aspects of the project by embedding it into project processes and sign offs

Delivery governance

Good governance should act as a risk management strategy for the organization and a support mechanism for the delivery team.

When an organization introduces project-based activity, governance processes structures and systems are developed and continue to mature as the cost and complexity of projects increases. In the early days informal approval and monitoring processes keep an eye on spending and progress. As the organization becomes more dependent on project activity, governance structures and processes are introduced to add formality, transparency and accountability. As these develop further they begin to take on a broader business focus integrating project governance into business forums and controls. Figure 4.3.4 below outlines a typical progression in delivery governance maturity and the template in Appendix 8 will help you identify your organization's current level of project governance maturity and the areas that need to be maintained or developed.

Whatever the level of maturity in your organization, good governance should act as a risk management strategy for the organization and a support mechanism for the delivery team. Those involved in governance must have a primarily business, not project, perspective supported by good strategic and analytical thinking skills. They must be actively engaged, fully informed, influential and supportive.

CASE STUDY   Successful change delivery

Prentice Healthcare understand that delivery is an important part of the story when it comes to organizational change. The leadership team have invested in a simple project management framework and toolset to provide some consistency in the way they manage projects. They have worked hard to ensure the framework is used consistently throughout the organization and delivers valuable outcomes. After many months of effort, their governance forums now make good-quality decisions quickly, remove obstacles and maintain a focus on the drivers and benefits.

In addition to their ability to successfully deliver a project on time and budget, project managers are recruited for their ability to lead people, manage relationships and be flexible. Project team members are recruited for their technical expertise and experience but also for their ability to deal effectively with the inevitable conflicts and uncertainty of the project lifecycle. They have succeeded in providing an environment where delivering on time, to budget and quality is treated with equal importance as preparing the environment for a smooth transition and benefits delivery.

Formal governance forums are kept to a minimum in favour of reliable and embedded control processes and regular contact between the sponsor, change manager, project manager and key stakeholders. This empowers business managers to make decisions and enables a more agile approach which maintains progress. Steering committee meetings are chaired by the project sponsor and have equal representation from project and business teams.

Figure 4.3.4 Delivery governance maturity level indicators

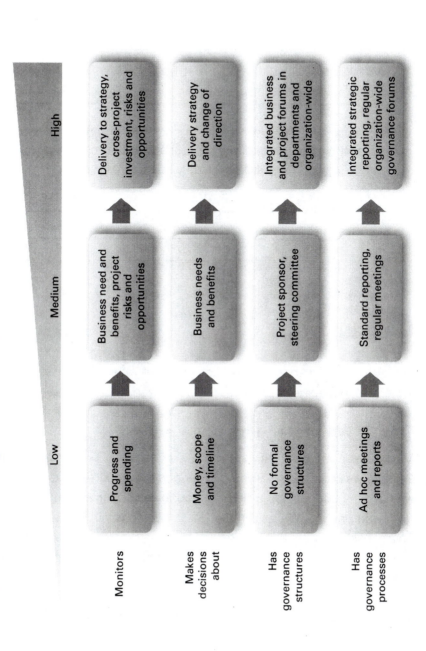

Low   Medium   High

Monitors — Progress and spending → Business need and benefits, project risks and opportunities → Delivery to strategy, cross-project investment, risks and opportunities

Makes decisions about — Money, scope and timeline → Business needs and benefits → Delivery strategy and change of direction

Has governance structures — No formal governance structures → Project sponsor, steering committee → Integrated business and project forums in departments and organization-wide

Has governance processes — Ad hoc meetings and reports → Standard reporting, regular meetings → Integrated strategic reporting, regular organization-wide governance forums

Think ...

1   My organization considers a change starts when

_____

and finishes when

_____

_____

2   Does my organization effectively and consistently use project structures (projects, programmes and portfolios) to aide successful delivery?

_____

_____

Deliver traps

Whilst project management may be a relatively mature discipline, it is still vulnerable to a range of problems if it is not used in the right way.

Trap 1: We pretend it's not a project

Maybe we don't want all the fuss associated with project governance. Perhaps we know our initiative won't support the organization's strategy but we have the budget, see a benefit to our own department and so want to go ahead anyway. We assign the job to people within the department to do alongside their usual role. We don't make anyone the project manager so that we can keep the initiative 'below the radar'. We hide it so well that we find it hard to track progress or expenditure.

Trap 2: We see project management as a temporary capability

If we see projects as individual temporary structures then we associate the capability to deliver change as a temporary need. When a project starts we struggle to find the best people, processes and tools for the job. Towards the end of the project specialists know they don't have a role after the change is implemented and start looking for their next job several weeks before the change goes live. Tools methods and project memory are lost as the team are dispersed thus making the establishment of the next project as hard as the last.

Trap 3: We don't involve the people impacted

For a variety of reasons we may not involve the people who are going to be asked to change. Perhaps we think they are too busy or that it's the project team's job to work things out. Perhaps we believe the expensive specialists we have recruited into the project team know best and that representatives from the business don't have the right experience to provide useful input to the solution design.

Sometimes we invite business subject matter experts to get involved but it's too late for them to have any influence over the design of the change and this just seems to increase frustration and resistance which ironically puts us off consulting them in the future. Whilst user-centric design and iterative and consultative methods have become more common in recent years, our project team may still have no real intention of adapting the design as a result of the data gathered during consultation. This breeds mistrust between our project team and the recipients of the change and makes them reluctant to input to the next project.

Trap 4: We treat our vendors like our enemies

It is easy to see how early contractual negotiations – between commercial negotiators, lawyers and sales people can be driven by a desire for each party to maximize and protect their individual benefit. Unfortunately this approach can continue throughout the project. Vendors are nervous of 'scope creep' as their margins have been reduced. The project team see them as inflexible and not focused on their needs. Despite the critical part they play in delivery they are excluded from key meetings and their access to information and stakeholders is restricted. At a personal level, vendor team members are made to feel like outsiders. Their ability to effectively play their part in the change without the key information and relationships they need is severely hampered.

Trap 5: We believe that 'change = project'

There is a lot more to changing an organization than just running some projects but when we can't see the bigger picture we put more and more pressure on our projects to deliver the other elements of the change. Our poor project manager is feeling the heat and is keen to help but projects *enable* benefits – they don't deliver them. With the best will in the world the project manager is not in a position to influence the many steps required to deliver benefits. There is more work to do, long after the project team have finished up. Project teams do not have the authority, longevity, skills, resources or motivation to control the way changes are adopted and embedded into the business.

> Projects don't deliver benefits – they enable them.

Trap 6: Our projects are driving the business

Perhaps a few projects have failed to deliver so we ramp up our project management and governance processes. We invest heavily in project management skills, methodologies and governance structures in a bid to improve the return on investment in our projects. Up to a point this helps to bring some transparency, consistency and reliability to the delivery but if we are not careful our project management and governance processes take on a life of their own and start to drive, instead of be driven by, the business.

We bring in specialists who know more about project management than our business and unless we manage them carefully they build project control mechanisms that are incompatible with the culture, nature and pace of change in our organization. We gain a false sense of comfort from our impressive methodologies toolkits governance structures and forums. They look great and give us a sense of control with lots of manuals, templates reports and meetings but if they are not supporting our organization's change agenda they could be doing more harm than good.

Trap 7: We reward outputs more than outcomes

> Poor project governance focuses more on project process than business outcomes.

Our passion to pursue 'best practice' has led to an overreliance on method-ologies and templates over reality and business outcomes. We become preoccupied with compliance to the project management processes and cease to monitor real progress. Our project deliverables are seen as an end in themselves, regardless of whether they support good decision making. For example, our impact assessment is signed off by the project manager as a completed project deliverable instead of by the impacted leaders as an acknowledgement of the impact the change will have on their team. This process focus in turn creates a culture which rewards people for speed over quality and 'doing' rather than thinking. Project documents are seen as an exercise in 'covering your a***' and doing *something* is seen as better than doing the *right* thing.

Trap 8: We are overoptimistic about the outcomes

As human beings we have a tendency to be overoptimistic about future outcomes. We overestimate the likelihood of positive events and under-estimate negative ones. This can lead to oversight of key risks which later ambush us and derail the change. We frequently experience delays caused by inaccurate planning and estimating. Our governance forums have made assumptions which turn out to be incorrect as it becomes clear they have failed to ask some of the tough questions along the way.

Trap 9: We don't know what's really going on

Perhaps our delivery governance has become too overbearing, unsuppor-tive or irrelevant. In this environment our project managers learn that giving their projects a 'green' healthy status in the weekly report (regardless of the true state of things) means they won't be scrutinized or punished. Risks and obstacles are covered up as the project manager feels they will be blamed for any delays or problems. If the steering committee members are remote from the change activity, fail to ask the right people the right questions or appear to be unsupportive the governance is unlikely to be effective.

Trap 10: We take our eye off the ball too early

'Today's problems come from yesterday's solutions' (Peter Senge, 1990).

Perhaps we are so focused on getting our solution implemented that we fail to organize an adequate handover to those who need to look after the change after implementation. We don't even start to look at handover teams, tasks and criteria until a few weeks prior to implementation. The people who will be responsible for nurturing and embedding the change get a clear message from the project team that they are keen to 'dump and run' as soon as possible – to close the project down and move on to the next one. Instead of treating those impacted like a customer we treat them as an annoying distraction from project closure tasks. When it becomes clear that our solution needs 'tweaking' before it can deliver the business outcome we need the project team and their budget are nowhere to be seen.

Think...

1   Which of these traps is holding back your change?

2   Which one, if you fixed it, would bring the greatest benefit?

Deliver ideas

So now you've identified the things that are holding you back what can you do to increase your chances of delivery success? Below are 10 ideas that will set your delivery up to succeed.

Idea 1: Shoulder to shoulder with the 'customer' throughout

If we were to build a house we would work closely with the people who would be living in it. We'd keep them in the loop all the way through, involve them in major decisions and use their views and ideas along with our expertise and experience to deliver the best house. The same principle applies to building change solutions. The relationship between the delivery team and the people receiving the change must be one of partnership in its truest sense. Whilst both groups are focused on the same outcome there must be an acknowledgement that the delivery team bring specialist skills and experience and the business has to be able to confidently adopt, embed and sustain the solution. When this is a close relationship with plenty of trust, transparency and collaboration, problems can be raised early and fixed before they become a roadblock. The side-by-side nature of this relationship implies that the two parties are integrated as much as possible.

Idea 2: Give power to the right people

Ultimately the people receiving the change are going to have control over whether it delivers the right outcomes so there's no point giving them something they don't want or can't make work. In organizations that change successfully the *direction* is clear, the *driver* has the best interest of the organization at heart and the people receiving the change are able to influence decisions about the solution and its implementation. The delivery team provide a range of alternative solutions that have the potential to deliver the benefits required and those on the receiving end have the power to decide which of these has the best chance of success in their environment. Similarly, the delivery team provide alternative implementation scenarios and the business decides which of these represents the least risk to their current operation and the success of the change.

Idea 3: Tell people when they don't have the power

For the people impacted by the change there's only one thing worse than not being consulted and that's spending time providing their input only to feel that their views didn't make a difference. You can save yourself from considerable objections down the line if you make it clear to those being consulted how much power they have. Do they have the power to make decisions, recommendations or just input their views and ideas for consideration? When they know how much influence their views can have they can invest an appropriate level of energy and expectation.

Idea 4: Focus on the attributes as well as the skills of your delivery team

Mature project management practices with a heavy reliance on tools and frameworks can attract people with a high need for structure, control and certainty – three things organizational change will never offer! Your project manager must be comfortable working in an uncertain environment whilst effectively leading their team to make meaningful progress. Likewise project team members need to be resilient and flexible so they can quickly realign their activities in the face of the inevitable changes and obstacles.

Idea 5: Keep your delivery team happy and healthy

Your delivery team are an important stakeholder group and must be treated as such. New team members should be fully inducted into the project to enable them to get up and running quickly and make the most of the initial enthusiasm most people have for a new job. As the project progresses regularly measure the satisfaction levels of the team against the key criteria required for effective teamwork; for example clear roles, adequate skills and resources, clear goals, open communication and trust.

The way you reward your project managers and their teams will create behaviours aligned to those standards so reward them for the behaviour you want to see: enabling benefits not just meeting time, quality and cost targets; delivery of business outcomes not just systems and solutions; flexibility and finding creative solutions and not giving up in the face of obstacles.

Idea 6: Use the right tool for the job

The project management frameworks, methodology and capability should be the right ones for the job. They should be aligned to the type, scale, drivers, pace and frequency of the change your organization needs. If you need to make incremental changes frequently then a cumbersome methodology is not going to support this. Equally if you are making a big investment in a significant change then informal governance processes and a simple toolkit is unlikely to provide the support you need. If your organization's survival is dependent on being able to respond rapidly to opportunities in the market you will need sufficient structure to guide effective delivery but sufficient flexibility to be able to deliver or change direction quickly. Put in the effort up front to ensure that the methods you plan to use support the change you need to make.

Idea 7: Integrate delivery activities into the broader change cycle

By all means maintain the project lifecycle but put this within a broader change cycle which reflects and sets expectations about the activities, energy and investment required before and after the project. Give projects the support they need with clear *direction* and sufficient *drive*. Ensure they hand over the solution to the *propagators* in a way that enables success. Your budgets and plans should extend beyond go-live for months or years if that is what it will take to sustainably realize the benefits the organization needs.

Idea 8: Put the right people in charge of governance

Whilst it can be tempting to put a bunch of finance and project people on the steering committee this puts the decision making in the wrong hands. Governance forums have responsibility for the solution, approach, resources and timing. They trade off different aspects of these when making decisions. In order to be effective the people making those decisions need a broad view across both the solution and the environment into which it is being implemented and to have accountability for the consequences. They also need a full and up-to-date view of the broader business context to enable them to introduce relevant new information and make the right decisions.

CASE STUDY   An effective steering committee

The region's schools had been given funding to upgrade classroom equipment and a steering committee had been formed to oversee the work. The committee was made up of the sponsor – the regional head of schools, a teacher from each of the four areas within the region, a finance manager, the project manager and a representative from the equipment supplier. As the project progressed they encountered a series of obstacles relating to the equipment or its installation. The project manager presented a series of alternative approaches to resolving the issues. Finance considered the financial implications of each option on the broader budget, the vendor covered the logistical implications of each solution and the head of schools and the teachers made the final decision. As the steering committee was made up of representatives from each of the parties involved in delivering and receiving the change decisions were made quickly, were practical and well supported.

Idea 9: Focus governance on the right things

Your delivery governance must be proactive not reactive – actively engaging with the project, its people and processes. Steering committees and project boards should support the delivery team – keeping an eye on the bigger picture and the end game; picking up new information, rewarding achievements, creating an environment where reporting can reflect reality and helping the team to deal with obstacles.

The scope of governance must cover the readiness of both the solution and the environment into which it will be implemented. This means that in addition to monitoring the progress of the solution the governance processes and forums must track the support levels among those impacted and the progress of change management tasks required to prepare them for the change. (You'll learn more about this in the next chapter.)

As we know 'what gets measured gets managed' so governance processes must value outcomes more than output. Reporting and decision making must encourage the delivery of benefits not deliverables. Making decision making transparent is a major way to reduce resistance to change. By consistently using the project benefits as the frame of reference for decision making you reinforce their importance and encourage your people to make the best decisions.

Idea 10: Consider an agile approach

Whilst the term 'agile' has been applied in recent years to a specific form of software development, the underlying meaning of the word can be applied to any change for which this approach could improve the outcome. For many changes it is impossible to design the perfect solution from scratch at the first attempt. Building one or more prototype solutions enables everyone involved and impacted to see it , try it, incorporate new information and suggest improvements. The important thing is to see that this agile or 'light on your feet' approach is an iterative process over a period of time. It will not suit all changes and should not be seen as an excuse to put inappropriate pressure on timelines.

Think...

1 Which of these ideas could help your organization?

2 Which one would give you the most benefit?

So...

When you know which *direction* you need to go in and you have sufficient *drive* for the journey it pays to make sure that you are going to stay on the right road, get to your destination as quickly as possible and with a smile on the customer's face.

1 Are the people impacted by our change involved in a meaningful way (ie truly able to influence decisions) throughout the project?

_____

_____

_____

_____

2 Does my organization have a project management framework and tools that *help* us deliver the type of change our organization needs?

_____

_____

_____

_____

3 Do we see evidence to suggest that our project governance people and processes are focused on *business* outcomes or *project* outcomes?

_____

_____

_____

_____

4 What can we do to improve the effectiveness of project delivery?

_____

_____

_____

_____

5 What can we do to improve the effectiveness of project governance? (Use the template in Appendix 8 to help you identify your organization's current level of project governance maturity and the areas that need to be maintained or developed.)

_____

_____

_____

_____

6 The most important thing I need to remember about *delivering* change is

_____

_____

_____

_____

Want to know more?

Search engine terms: project management, programme management, port-folio management, project governance, project planning, project manager.

Prepare for the change

Prepare: To make ready beforehand for a specific purpose, as for an event or occasion

Without the right preparation you will not deliver the benefits your organization needs.

Figure 4.4   Prepare for the change

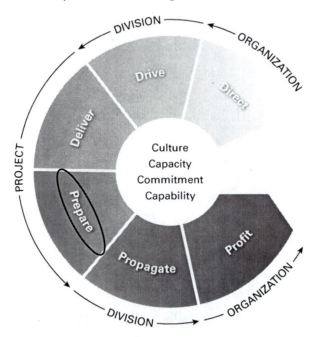

Successful organizations prepare for change. They ensure everything that needs to be in place to support a change is ready by the time it is delivered. They place a strong focus on preparing both internal and external people and environments so that change can be adopted and embedded as easily as possible. Indeed this concept of 'readiness' is at the heart of the need to *prepare* an organization for change.

Organizations invest in major improvements because they see a need to do, be or provide something different. It therefore follows that the majority of changes will not fit neatly and easily into the current environment. The processes, systems, skills, knowledge and behaviour required to make the change successful are unlikely to already exist and the environment will need to adapt to get ready for the change. Imagine you have a strategy to implement a 'square peg' but your organization only has 'round holes'. Either the peg and/or the hole will need to compromise if the change is to be successful. This concept of the change 'fitting' the environment to ensure a smooth transition is critical to *preparing* the organization for change.

Mature organizations understand they need to be in a constant state of readiness: not just for the next change but any change. We saw in Chapter 3 how important it is to continually build a culture, commitment, capacity and capability for change within your organization. Now that you have a specific change in mind you can ramp up these activities and focus on the specific impacts and interventions.

So what do you need to prepare? There are two things that will impede the success of any change once it is delivered. The first and maybe most obvious is your people – their knowledge, skills, attitudes, assumptions, hopes, fears and beliefs. As many of these as possible need to be aligned to support your change *before* it is delivered. Preparation activities also need to make ready the non-human elements of the environment into which the change is being introduced. These may include policies, procedures, standards, measures, technology, tools, structure and resources.

Preparing your people

Change cannot start without a critical level of support so preparing people for change starts right at the outset. In the early stages leaders must be *ready* to listen, understand, advocate for the change and provide resources. As the change progresses the impacted people (change recipients) must be *ready* to contribute effectively to the design and the leaders *ready* to make decisions. As you approach implementation you'll need to prepare people for the new way of working. Through all stages of the change managers need to be ready to lead their team. Figure 4.4.1 provides a summary of the typical outcomes you should be aiming for from your preparation activities.

Figure 4.4.1   People readiness

	Before Change	During Change	After Change
Change Recipients	'I am ready to listen, understand and get involved'	'I am ready to change the way I work'	'I am ready to "keep at it" and pursue the path required of me'
Change Leaders	'I am ready to listen, understand, commit, get involved and lead my team'	'I am ready to lead my team to adopt, embed and sustain the change'	'I am ready to "keep at it" and pursue the path required of me and my team until benefits are realized'

Each person's view of the change will depend on their perception of the impact. To one person it will look small and harmless and to another it will look huge and dangerous; one person will think its great whilst another will think its dreadful. Some people will not like the new way of working and others will react to the pain of the transition. Some may appear to support it one day and resist it the next. Some will have seemingly irrational attachments to elements that the change is designed to remove. For example, stopping production of a product that consumers are no longer buying makes good business sense but your people may have put years of effort into that product and identify strongly with it.[20] Not everyone will resist and you must be ready to reward those who are supporting the change as well as support those who are more fearful. Welcome to the world of change management and change leadership!

People's reactions will be influenced by their previous experience, personality and resilience levels but humans are hardwired to see change as a threat so some level of resistance is to be expected no matter how popular the outcome. David Rock in his work on neuro-leadership (2009) gives us the SCARF model to explain how it is natural for us to react badly to change in the first instance. He explains how our primitive brain is triggered by a perceived threat to our sense of status, certainty, autonomy, relatedness and fairness. We have a natural aversion to loss which leads us to feel risks more acutely than op-portunities and makes us prefer the status quo over any changes. When change triggers fear inertia sets in as we look for evidence to support our fears and disregard evidence that does not fit our picture of doom and gloom. We seek out examples that justify our fears – maybe a previous change handled badly.

So it's normal for everyone impacted (yes – even the boss!) to feel shocked, angry, frustrated and fearful when they are asked to change. When preparing your people you are not trying to prevent these emotions – they're normal. What you are trying to do is to move your people through that stage as quickly as possible. Only when they have come to accept the change will they listen to what you have to say and chose to get on board.

'If you wish to persuade me you must think my thoughts, feel my feelings and speak my words' (Marcus Tullius Cicero, 106-43BCE).

Given our natural tendency to be suspicious or fearful of changes, and the poor track record of organizational change, it is clear that preparing our people is a significant task and one that requires a constant focus from the very beginning to the very end of a change. The good news is there is plenty of research out there to help explain why people resist change and you can use this to guide the activities you'll need. At its simplest preparing your people should aim to build their confidence. Everybody's needs vary but your activities should create confidence that:

- they will maintain their dignity and self-esteem throughout;
- they will have some control over the outcome or the method to get there;
- their time is well spent;
- their voices will be heard and acted upon;
- they will be capable of doing what they need to do;
- the future will be okay or better;

- the outcomes are valued by people whose opinion matters;
- the gains will outweigh the pains;
- the investment is worthwhile.

Only when this is achieved can you expect people to effectively play the role you need them to to make your change successful.

Preparing your people is an unpredictable task and getting it 100 per cent right for everyone is nigh on impossible. Decide what the tipping point is for your change. Maybe having 51 per cent of the people supportive is enough to get it across the line or perhaps you need 75 per cent. As people adopt the change, if it is well designed, managed and implemented, their support will increase to enable you to realize your benefits.

Preparing your environment

It's not just people that resist change. Few if any changes exist in isolation. Most will sit alongside existing processes systems artefacts and practices and will have ripple effects on those or vice versa. Change can only be adopted and embedded efficiently when it 'fits' the environment into which it is being introduced. If we don't address the surrounding environment, for example the physical surroundings, interrelated policies, processes, measures and systems we may not see the impact they are having on our change until it is too late. Consider the examples outlined in Figure 4.4.2 and 4.4.3 below and how the environment helped or hindered the successful adoption of four changes.

Figure 4.4.2   Change fails when it conflicts with its surroundings

An energy company deployed a new call handling system to cut call waiting times for customers	BUT	...15% of calls required the operator to use another system which was unable to meet the new service levels
A government department wanted their IT team to have a more user-centric approach	BUT	...their KPIs rewarded technical performance and delivery to technical deadlines

The first example shows how a singular focus on a project goal, without taking into account the bigger picture, means this change was undermined from

Day One as there was no way the operators could meet the goals set. In the second example you can see how asking the team to be more 'user-centric' but still measuring their performance in terms of technical delivery sends mixed messages. If their bonus is linked to the achievement of their KPIs it's easy to work out which behaviours you are most likely to see!

Figure 4.4.3   Change succeeds when it fits its surroundings

A not-for-profit organization wanted to introduce a more commercial focus	AND	...all policies were redrafted to support the new approach
An engineering company wanted to introduce a less hierarchically based culture	AND	...they removed all individual offices and managers sat with their teams

By contrast Figure 4.4.3 illustrates how easily a change can be sustained if the environment into which it is implemented is adapted to support it. In the first example the not-for-profit organization wanted to bring about a major shift in their business model. As they worked their way through the design they realized the majority of the organization's policies would prevent the new model from working as intended and they would need to be redrafted. The updated policies sent a strong message to their stakeholders about the importance of the change. In the second example removing the physical symbols of hierarchy is clearly a good step if you want to remove the negative effects of a hierarchical culture. By forcing a change in behaviour it sends a strong message about how 'real' and important the cultural change is.

Change management

Whilst project management ensures successful change *delivery*, change management is the professional discipline you'll need to make sure everything and everyone is ready to receive the change. There are many good books on change management and this chapter will not seek to cover the topic in detail. What it will do is explain the scope and nature of the activities you'll need to consider and provide some insights into the type of people who can help you prepare your business for change.

> Change management within a project is the structured and systematic approach to making the people and the environment ready to adopt and sustain change.

Just as we saw the effects of increasing project management maturity your organization's level of change management maturity will also impact greatly on your chances of success.[21] The Change Management Institute's Organisational Change Management Maturity Model shows how in the early stages an organization will primarily focus on training and communication activities in support of change implementation. As maturity develops change management is applied earlier in the lifecycle and the use of specialist change management resources increases. Subsequently the scope and formality grow and change management activity is integrated into project and business processes. Not everyone needs to aim for full maturity. Your change will be successful when the level and nature of change management maturity is aligned to the nature and rate of future change in your organization. For most organizations the scope of change management should include the following:

Manage stakeholder relationships. Continually identifying and assessing the level of support from everyone inside and outside of the organization who is (or believes they may be) impacted by the development or implementation of the change. Planning and executing strategies to build and maintain the required level of commitment.

Communicate and engage. Developing and communicating core messages. Understanding the needs of all stakeholders and making the right information available through a variety of channels at the right time. Providing meaningful feedback mechanisms to build and validate understanding.

Measure monitor and fix. Continually identifying and mitigating people and sustainability risks. Providing lead and lag measures of progress, readiness and effectiveness throughout and acting on the findings.

Define the change. Developing a clear and concise definition of the drivers, scope, timeline and benefits of the change which is used to build a consistent understanding.

Understand the environment. Having a good understanding of the environment into which the change will be implemented: the elements that will support the change and those that will get in the way and will therefore need to be avoided or adapted.

Understand the impact. Understanding the impact the change will have on the various internal and external stakeholders. At a high level building an awareness of the 'hot spots' and at a detailed level understanding what each individual role will need to do, be or know, that is different from today.

Develop and execute a change strategy and a plan. These documents outline how the business and its people will be prepared for and supported through the change. The strategy and the plan must outline the approach and activities required in areas such as leadership, sustainability, communication, organizational changes, training and support.

Note that whilst this list may imply a sense of sequence it is important to remember that many of these tasks will be iterative as the understanding of the change and its impact develops.

Change manager

The Change Management Institute's Change Management Practitioner Competency Model provides an excellent outline of the activities required to prepare a business for change and therefore what you should expect to see from your change manager.[22] As well as a basic understanding of project management, facilitation, training and communications it covers topics such as environmental analysis, strategic thinking and coaching. Depending on the scale and nature of the change a change manager is often supported by specialists in communications, training, human resources and organization development. Although they are often part of the project team their allegiance is always to the people on the receiving end of the change and they represent their interests and views throughout. Change managers come from a wide range of backgrounds but must have five critical personal characteristics:

- Self-awareness and management. Dealing with people's emotions every day can be a daunting task. A good change manager understands and manages their own emotional reactions so they are in a position to understand and deal with others'.

- Empathy. The ability to suspend their own viewpoint, look at things from the perspective of a wide range of people and use this information to tailor their approach.

- Humility. Not too much and not too little but sufficient to enable all stakeholders to respect and relate to them.

- Resilience. The role of the change manager is to stand with one foot in the delivery camp and one foot in the receiving camp, serving two masters. Depending on the relationship between the project and the business, this can be a tough role. Often they are taking unwelcome news either into the project or the business. They usually have little or no authority and can often burn out from the strain of finding effective ways to gain the influence they need.

- Flexibility. Organizational change creates ambiguity and the change manager will be surrounded by fearful people looking for certainty. They must be comfortable working in this 'grey' area.

CASE STUDY   A great change manager

Lucy was a great change manager. She had started her career in training before developing an appetite for being involved earlier in the cycle and managing the other aspects of the change. She had already managed several large changes so knew what to expect when she started her new role as change manager for a new customer relationship management system at a large accounting firm.

Her first task was to provide input to the business case; making sure all the benefits were clearly articulated, links to the strategy were clear and that there was sufficient time and money in the plan to support the change management activities. This work helped her understand who had been engaged to date and who was making the decisions. Then she made contact with everyone who had been involved and worked with them to identify the full range of internal and external groups impacted; their influence, needs, preferences, hot buttons and levels of support. Having allocated a relationship owner to each of the important stakeholders she set up the mechanisms to monitor and manage

Figure 4.4.4 Change management project plan

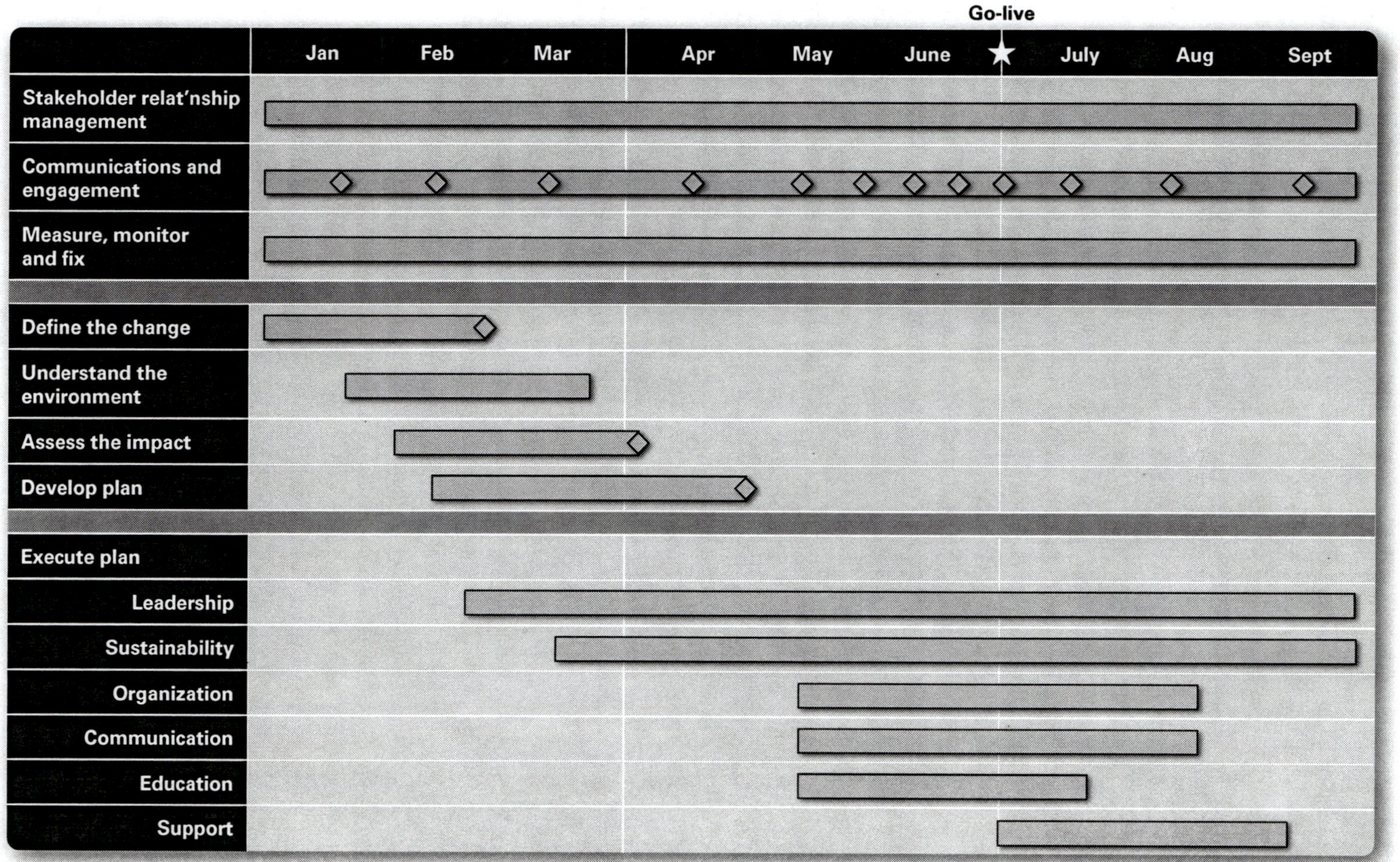

these throughout. Next she worked with the internal communications and public affairs team to develop a plan outlining how and when each stakeholder would be engaged and put this into action.

In parallel with this Lucy developed the project plan of her activities (see Figure 4.4.4) and a budget for each stage of the change as she would need to integrate these into the broader project planning.

She knew the size of the budget she'd need would depend on the scale and impact of the change and the nature of the environment it was impacting. She gathered some high-level information about the range and number of impacted people and locations, the scale and type of impact on each group, their current change readiness and likely barriers to commitment. Given the scale of the change she would need to allow for a training manager and a budget for communications collateral.

Next she went out into the impacted business units to find out whatever she could that would help her decide the right approach to preparing those teams for the new system. She asked about their culture and current way of working so that she could plan to leverage the helpful aspects and mitigate the hindering aspects of the environment. She asked about previous changes as she knew she'd have to overcome any change 'skeletons' before she could gain their commitment. She gathered information about the people in the teams – where they worked, working hours, age range and other demographic information as she knew she'd have to develop a communications plan that worked for everyone.

By the time she had done this the delivery team were ready to design the new processes and system so she helped them involve the right people from the client management teams. She knew this consultation would be critical to gaining their support for the change and that it would help the IT team understand how the system would be used. Lucy also knew that it would be an important part of making sure the system was easy to adopt and sustain. She knew it was never too early to think about life after the implementation and she was pretty sure the rest of the delivery team were too busy with the system to think too much about it just yet.

As the solution design progressed Lucy worked with representatives from both the delivery team and the business teams to identify the scale and nature of impact on each role. The business needed to understand the scale and timing of the impact on their teams and Lucy needed to understand what they would be doing differently so she could help them develop the new skills, knowledge and mindsets they'd need to be successful.

She had already started to develop her change plan by the time the programme business owner signed off the impact assessment but now the solution was clear and the impacts largely identified Lucy could get on with listing all the things she would need to put in place to prepare them for the change. She knew she'd need some help from the experts and so worked with the human resources, internal communications, learning and development and organizational development teams to identify all the tasks she would need to do including:

- leadership activities;
- activities to ensure the change would be adopted and sustained easily;
- changes to role descriptions, performance targets and team structures;
- targeted and tailored communication to those impacted;
- a variety of tailored training activities and materials;
- post-implementation support for all aspects of the change;
- measures of success.

Lucy had set herself a firm foundation and she was ready to make it happen!

A common response from organizations that have invested heavily in project management is that they believe rightly or wrongly that the project manager already does the preparation work required. So can a project manager do the job of a change manager? The answer is 'probably as well as a plumber could do an electrician's job'. Whilst the disciplines are related, the skills, knowledge, activities, attributes, tools and goals are quite different. You wouldn't trust the plumber to rewire your house but you might let them rewire a plug. If the stakes are relatively low, and you have a project manager with the right attributes then there is no reason why they can't do a reasonable job.

> Change is made to measure not 'off the peg'.

Every change plan is different. Every workplace contains a unique landscape of human and non-human elements that need to be ready to receive the changes. Each change will impact some elements more than others. Further complicate this with the fact that every individual is different and will react differently dependent on a range of factors over which you have no control and you'll see why changing organizations is so hard.

Think...

1 Who is responsible for making sure the people receiving our change are ready?

_____

_____

_____

2 What elements of our environment will need to be adapted if the change is going to 'fit' easily?

_____

_____

_____

Prepare traps

Whilst it makes sense to prepare your business to receive change, there are many things we may be doing to undermine this critical step in the change cycle.

Trap 1: We assume the business is ready

We neglect to prepare the people impacted by the change and assume leaders know what they need to do and are capable of doing it. How many times have you heard the phrase 'they just lobbed it over the wall' from business people impacted by major changes? This has two key words which sum up how many business people often feel about the way change is introduced. A dictionary definition of the verb 'to lob' is 'to fire (a missile, as a shell) in a high trajectory so that it drops onto a target.' In this case the target is a department full of people trying to do their job. The fact they see a 'wall' is also telling. They perceive the solution to be built out of sight and they only see it as it appears over the wall. It also implies that the project team stay behind the wall and don't come to the business side to see the effects of their 'lobbing'. Equally the business people never go to the project side of the wall to check that what they are building is what they need and work out what they need to do to get ready for it.

Trap 2: We expect our staff and customers to commit to the change easily

It all makes perfect sense to us and we can't understand why they wouldn't agree! Humans are hardwired to react to change and also to surprises. Projects that get close to implementation before discussing the changes with the people on the receiving end are guaranteed to see resistance even when the outcome is positive. People feel ambushed and take a while to absorb the information and work out the impacts. It is unlikely that you will be able to effectively address this reaction *and* get them ready to adopt and embed the change effectively in the short time available. As leaders we forget that we have had months to understand and influence the change and it is this that has led to us being so comfortable and confident.

Trap 3: We believe the delivery team is taking care of everything

Everything about the delivery team is focused on *delivery* – designing, building, testing and deploying the right solution. The meetings, reports, governance, skills and experience of the team members are focused on delivery and are unlikely to be focused on preparing the business teams that will take on the change. Organizations with lower levels of change maturity treat change management as a subset of project management. This naturally symbolizes that delivery of the solution is more important than preparing well for the change to be received. The needs of the project (delivering on time and budget) quickly overrule the needs of the business (an easy transition of a sustainable solution which delivers benefits). A survey by a project management professional body showed that 72 per cent of project managers believed that change management was a subset of project management.[23] There is clearly more work to do in this area!

Trap 4: We only provide training and communication

We may think that some training and communication at 'go-live' is all that's required to prepare our people for what is coming. Often this rather naive approach is associated with a limited view of both training and communication. We consider our obligation is met when the e-mail is sent and the training courses posted online. We don't consider whether the messages have been opened, read, understood or acted on and we have no idea whether the training has built the capability and confidence required to support the change.

Training and communications are critical but will not be effective unless they are received by people who are ready to take on board the information and willing to do what is required of them. People impacted by change have a complex range of fears and emotions and communications and training alone will not address these significant roadblocks. Humans rarely, if ever, change their beliefs or have their fears allayed as result of an e-mail or an online training module!

Trap 5: We ignore the impact of the environment on our change

Perhaps we are so focused on designing and building the right solution we take on a sort of tunnel vision. Even if we get clues along the way that tell us there will be problems embedding the change we try to ignore these signs in favour of meeting our delivery deadlines. Perhaps we don't know how to identify those elements of the current environment that will conflict with and therefore disrupt our change. How can we expect our people to change the way they do things if their performance targets, policies, systems, physical surroundings, artefacts, processes or norms encourage them otherwise?

Trap 6: We expect people to fit into our structured delivery frameworks

There can sometimes be tensions between the structured and deadline driven approach to delivery and the somewhat erratic nature of managing human reactions that is involved with preparing the people for change. A project manager may insist that change management deliverables are completed as stated in the methodology and the project plan. The change manager has to work with the reality of current levels of understanding and buy-in within the business. This often means activities have to be reprioritized to adapt deliverables and their timing to suit the needs of the audience rather than the needs of the delivery team, governance and methods. For example, if a senior stakeholder is not 'ready' to sign off the impact assessment there will inevitably be a delay to the change plan that is dependent on it.

Trap 7: The effectiveness of our change management activities is undermined

When our business units do not understand the tasks required to engage their commitment and make them ready for a change they may ignore attempts to prepare them. If past changes have largely left them alone until implementation they may be suspicious of attempts to engage them early no matter how honourable your intentions. Our delivery teams can also inadvertently undermine the success of the change by restricting access to critical project information, forums and resources; leaving all the engagement up to the change manager; refusing to involve impacted people in a meaningful way or conveying a sense of frustration with seemingly erratic stakeholder views and opinions.

Trap 8: We don't spend any money on preparation

We've invested millions in the design and delivery of the new system but baulk at the small amount of money needed to print 'cheat sheets' and posters. We have 50 IT people working on the delivery team but question the need to bring in one change manager and an instructional designer. We clearly believe that 'delivering change' is much more important than 'receiving change'.

Trap 9: We start our preparation too late

We don't think we need to 'bother' the business until we are closer to implementation so we go about our project business, making decisions, getting the solution ready. When we start our implementation activity we are horrified at the lack of buy-in (how ungrateful they are for all the work we've done on their behalf!). We find a host of things we didn't know about which will impact on the success of the solution but it's too late to change it.

Trap 10: We see change management activities as 'nice to have'

In other words we don't think they have a tangible business value. We think briefings and consultation are purely aimed at making people feel good and this seems like a luxury in our 'cut and thrust' business. We don't consider the fact that without good preparation the people and the environment will not be ready, productivity will plummet, the change will fail, we won't get our benefits and the millions we have invested will be wasted. Oh and it'll be much harder to embark on more change in the future!

> Think...
>
> 1 Which of these traps is holding back your change?
>
> 2 Which one, if we fixed it, would bring the greatest benefit?

Prepare ideas

So now you've discovered some of the things that are holding you back from preparing your business for change, what are some of the idea you can use right now to improve your chances of success?

Idea 1: Build a constant state of readiness in the business

Set the expectation of your people that change is here to stay and build business capability to lead, adopt and sustain those changes. Something as simple as explaining to new recruits that they will be asked to constantly adapt and take on new skills and processes can go a long way to reducing resistance. Leadership development must focus on the manager's role in maintaining the expectations and agility of their team and their ability to easily integrate business improvements.

Helping people to understand how and why they react to change and provide tools and strategies to help them deal with it makes good business sense. It encourages and equips all staff to help them manage their own reactions – thus reducing the stress people feel and the pressure on managers to 'do something to fix it'. Providing this support to everyone in the organization (yes – even the executive!) can send a powerful message about the need to embed this capability as well as give the organization a common language to help them manage resistance.

Idea 2: Understand and apply change management disciplines

Create an environment where preparation activities are valued and supported. This may mean educating the business and the delivery teams and assigning a senior sponsor from both areas to champion the change management work in its early days. Recruit or develop experts in change management to help you build capability. Make everybody responsible for business readiness by encouraging everyone in the project team to build and maintain the trust and confidence of the impacted people. Source or develop an appropriate change management framework and toolset which delivers consistently good outcomes across the range of changes your organization is likely to need. Integrate the project and change management frameworks so they can work in partnership to acknowledge and plan for the interdependencies. Use the full range of change levers available to you by including leadership, operating model, organization and role changes and a focus on sustainability in your preparation activities.

Idea 3: Make 'receiving' as important as 'delivering'

We know that one without the other will not work. If the solution is ready and the business isn't the change will fail. If the business is ready and the solution isn't the change will fail. Both are therefore equally important and you must symbolize this in the way you approach change. Your project manager and change manager should be peers – each leading their side of the equation. Spending should reflect an equal balance of resources on both sides. Governance forums and processes should give equal attention to monitoring the progress and risks of both delivering and receiving the change. By giving equal status you demonstrate that successful change is a partnership between delivering and receiving change – working together with the common goal of building a solution which works in the environment in which it is to be deployed and is able to sustainably deliver benefits.

Idea 4: Role-play the change

Ask the impacted people to role-play themselves in the new world and you'll soon identify where some of your barriers might be. They will quickly identify ripple effects the change will create and help you work out what to do about them. For example, if you ask a bank employee to role-play the new credit card application process they will quickly tell you whether the customer behaviour that is assumed in the process is realistic. They'll also be able to tell you how the new procedure fits with the other processes that are typically conducted at the same time. Perhaps the banker will need to collect the same customer information twice or a customer is unlikely to have easy access to some of the information. They will have valuable ideas about how the process can be adapted to make it easier for bankers and customers to adopt the change which you'd be wise to heed.

Idea 5: Articulate the consequences of not aligning your environment

It's not always possible to change everything we'd like to to enable a change to 'fit'. If you know there are elements of the environment you'd like to change but for whatever reason can't then use the governance processes to raise awareness of this risk and its consequences with the steering committee so that they make a fully informed decision.

CASE STUDY   Making critical decisions

The regulatory compliance team of Trent Investment Bank were in the final stages of designing the new branch process to identify new customers. The change manager was keen to add a KPI to everyone's performance measures along the lines of 'Fully comply with all regulatory obligations'. They felt this would give it constant focus and provide sufficient personal consequences to ensure the bankers stuck to the new process. The human resources department however was embedding a new performance management system and was not keen on changing KPIs mid-year. The change manager took the following decision to the steering committee:

Decision required: Will we update people's KPIs to include compliance with regulatory processes?

Rationale: The new processes may appear cumbersome in the early stages. In addition to leadership support and a full communications and training programme, providing personal consequences for non-compliance is a strong way of ensuring the new processes are carried out reliably and the bank is compliant in the eyes of the regulator.

Options:

A Update the KPIs at the time of implementation

B Update the KPIs at the next annual cycle

C Do not include a reference to compliance in banker KPIs

The knock-on effects and relative advantages and disadvantages of each option were discussed and, after hearing from the head of HR, the steering committee opted for option B whilst acknowledging and accepting the risk this would represent to the short-term success of the change and indeed the bank's regulatory compliance.

Idea 6: No surprises

If there is one strategy that applies to all changes it's this one – 'no surprises'. Even good change can feel bad if we are ambushed by it. People need plenty of time and information to understand how they feel about a change. Those impacted will need to listen, absorb what they have heard, try out the new ways, understand what it means to them and then integrate it into their world.[24] People will go through this journey at different speeds and react in different ways but everyone will benefit from plenty of opportunity to understand the need to change, observe and reflect on what they need to do, think about what it means for them and how they will go about it before giving it a go. In practical terms this means starting to talk about the change as early as possible (even when you haven't got most of the answers), providing plenty of two-way communication, creating opportunities for people to see and try the new way in a time, a way and at a pace that suits their needs.[25]

CASE STUDY   Preparing for an office relocation

West City Media were moving their head office to a new building on the edge of the town. During the construction phase the staff were kept up to date with messages and videos about the construction. As soon as the building was accessible, but long before the move, the project team fitted out one area of a floor with the new workspace furniture and features such as creative spaces and hot desks. During the final months of construction there were regular trips organized for teams to come and see the new building, understand and get used to their new journey to work, try out the new workspaces, ask questions and provide suggestions. A few weeks before their move, each team would visit their workspace, be encouraged to plan how they would use the new facilities and work out who would sit where. This gave everyone a chance to get used to the change at their own pace. By the time they moved in everyone was confident and optimistic and the inevitable teething troubles were resolved quickly and easily.

Change naturally brings uncertainty so the strategy of 'no surprises' is aimed at appealing to our brain's natural affinity for a feeling of control. You can create opportunities for impacted people to feel in control by giving them choices. It's a bit like the mum who asks her three year-old whether she wants to wear the blue trousers or the green trousers. The child is focused on the options provided, fully engaged and in control of which trousers she wears. (Left to her own devices she may have wanted to wear the torn black trousers but Mum's clever strategy avoids a tantrum!) Depending on the driver, scope and timeline of the change there may be few or many opportunities to build in choices for the people on the receiving end of the change. During design of a new system they can vote for their favourite screen layout. When they need to go to training they can choose the session, location or method. If the change allows they may be able to choose when they 'go-live'. Build in as many choices for those impacted as possible throughout the change to provide that reassuring sense of control.

> The shift from 'if we change' to 'when we change' is a powerful one that helps people move on from resistance to acceptance.

Idea 7: Expect and plan for resistance

Not everyone will resist the change but someone inevitably will. Resistance may take the active form (they are complaining to you or their colleagues about the change) or passive (whilst they are espousing support their actions make it clear they have no intention of doing what you need them to do!). Whichever form it takes you'll need to find out what they are resisting and why. It may be an unjustified fear or they may have valuable information about why the change will not be a success. Whether they are your 'constant complainers' (the people who always seem to resist everything) or this is the only time you have seen them actively resist an initiative – they are a godsend and you should listen to your greatest critics – at least for a while.

Often resistant people start out by not wanting to talk to you. They don't turn up for meetings; every attempt to engage them is met with an increase in their resistance. Dealing with people who are in a highly charged emotional state and who reject you constantly is a tough but necessary part of the change leader's job. Be patient and when you find a time and a way to talk to them constructively they will share their concerns (real or imagined). A good change manager, in conjunction with the person's line manager, can validate or mitigate those fears and help the person move on through the change towards acceptance. In a large number of cases people just want to be heard and an opportunity to share their expectations and fears can be enough to significantly reduce their resistance.

You'll also need to know when to stop giving the resisters your attention. For most changes there are a few people who will always resist no matter what you say or do. After a while they become the 'squeaky wheel' and if you're not careful you can be seen by them and others to be rewarding resistant behaviour. The trick is to give them enough support and attention to enable them to help themselves then focus your attention on those supporting or trying to support the change.

Change starts with you

As leaders we often think we can't or shouldn't react badly to a change but even when you are leading a change it's normal to have a range of positive and negative reactions. Learning to overcome these quickly and take a more constructive approach is critical if you are going to confidently lead your people through the change.

Idea 8: Communicate, communicate, communicate

Clear and consistent communication is the backbone of the activities required to develop and maintain trust and confidence. It is a hard one to get right as everyone needs and expects something different but as far as possible communicate in a way that suits your audience and their needs. This may seem obvious but many change programmes become absorbed in their own world and plan and execute their communication from their own standpoint – 'we want to tell them' rather than 'our audience want to hear'.

Keep repeating the basics. Focus on the facts and create as much certainty as you can: why your organization is changing and why now... what is changing... what's not changing... how it will impact which people and what success looks like. The programme team may be familiar with the drivers, scope and benefit of the change but your audience probably aren't. People's attention will come and go, new stakeholders will become involved. Every significant communication or interaction with a stakeholder should start with a recap of your elevator pitch. Even if you think your stakeholder has heard it before – say it again.

Whilst formal communication programmes are important, messages are sent every day about your change by the people working on it and these must be consistent. Your project team members (including external consultants and vendors) should have heard it so often that they can repeat it accurately and consistently to anyone they come into contact with. Remember that when communicating face to face the words you use are only a fraction of the message your people receive. Take care to ensure that your body language and tone of voice are consistent with the message. Finally, always provide a self-service source of further information and tell people where they can go if they have questions.

Idea 9: Use your informal networks

Successful organizational change finds the path of least resistance. You already know that the informal communication network in your organization is the quickest way of spreading a message so why not use it? Find out who is influential in this network. Who do people listen to and believe? Who do they seek out to validate or discuss their fears? Who has regular contact with a large number of people in the organization? These are the people whose views you should seek and who's support you will need to gain to maintain an open two-way flow of information throughout the organization. These people are obviously a natural choice for your network of change champions too – the group you bring 'into the tent' every so often throughout the project to share information and seek feedback.

Here's an example that illustrates the need to influence informal as well as formal channels. The following conversation was overheard on a plane between two air stewardesses. 'I saw the e-mail from head office and just wanted to check it out...' In other words – I've seen the facts, I'm just trying to work out what I think about it and your view will influence my view.

Idea 10: Monitor and measure everything

37 per cent either don't measure change or they don't know if they do or feel measuring change is too difficult (Nick Anderson and Kelly Nwosu, 2012).

If you think preparation outcomes are intangible think again. Just about everything can be measured and you'll need these measurements to tell you whether your efforts are having the desired effect and your valuable resources are being spent on the right things. Preparation is usually monitored and managed through the risk log and its associated governance processes. Figure 4.4.5 shows how this was done in the earlier example where the change manager wanted to change the bankers' KPIs.

Figure 4.4.5 Risk log

There is a risk that...	Like-lihood	Impact	Owner	Status	Mitigation Plan
The bank may not remain compliant if we are unable to align banker's KPIs	M	H	Mary Jones	Decision pending with steering committee	If we are unable to change banker KPIs we can (a) Visibly celebrate and reward compliance and (b) Implement random quarterly compliance checks to encourage bankers to continue to follow the process

When it comes to monitoring your internal and external stakeholder readiness you should measure the following components:

- Effectiveness of engagement activities. For example data and verbatim comments to illustrate levels of understanding and commitment among key groups and individuals and a measure of the volume and type of questions being received through feedback channels.
- Effectiveness of communication activities showing whether they achieved the outcome they needed to.
- Effectiveness of training activities providing evidence that people have developed the required level of confidence and competence.

Think...

1 Which of these ideas could help your organization?

2 Which one would give you the most benefit?

So...

You've got a clear *direction*, a *driver* with enough energy to see it through and a strong *delivery* capability but how well *prepared* are you and your organization for the change? The template in Appendix 9 will enable you to conduct a high-level impact assessment and develop an appropriate change strategy for each of your impacted stakeholder groups. The following questions will help you identify some broader areas for consideration.

1 Are our leaders ready to visibly support the change?

_____

_____

_____

_____

2 Do the people impacted by the change understand the impact it will have and the support they will receive to prepare for and embed the change?

_____

_____

_____

_____

3 Would the people impacted by the change say they felt fully informed, supported and confident?

_____

_____

_____

_____

4 Do we have a suitable change management framework and tools that help us prepare for the type of change our organization needs?

_____

_____

_____

_____

5 Is there a plan in place and budget allocated to prepare the change recipients and the environment for the change?

_____

_____

_____

_____

6 The most important thing I need to remember about _preparing_ for change is

_____

_____

_____

_____

Want to know more?

Search engine terms: change management, change manager, behaviour change, environmental scan, communicating change, stakeholder management, organizational development, learning and development, change readiness.

Propagate
the change

Propagate: to spread from person to person; disseminate

If you don't propagate your change you will not deliver the benefits
your organization needs.

Figure 4.5   Propagate the change

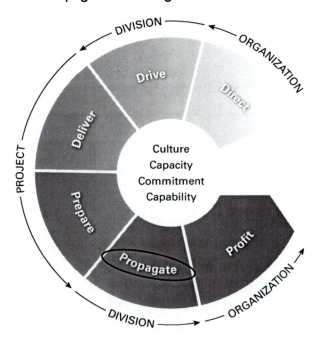

Successful organizations propagate their changes. They support their people,
land changes safely, make sure they stick and fix them if they don't. They
keep a close eye on them in the early days to make sure they are accepted,

adopted and embedded. If there are problems they fix them as quickly as possible to give the change the best chance of survival.

Smart organizations increase the energy after implementation to start the next phase of the change cycle. They understand that the change, business benefits and return on their considerable investment are rarely achieved on Day One. They know that asking their leaders and their teams to adopt and embed a new way of working requires constant vigilance, energy and resources. They understand that without this they will slip back to their old ways and if they do that their organization will slip back too.

If you think about a new change as being like a seedling you'll see how fragile your change is at this stage. If you dropped the seedling on the ground and hoped for the best you are extremely likely to get nothing in return. Alternatively if you prepare the soil, weed, feed and water it, protect it from pests and extreme elements and keep up this level of care over a long period that delicate seedling will become a strong tree that can look after itself and, indeed, begin to provide support for other elements.

A word about the word... the word propagate seems to be falling out of common usage. You could use 'embed' or 'integrate' but only 'propagate' adequately implies the level of care and nurturing required to get a fragile change to stick to the extent you need to sustainably deliver benefits.

There are two compelling reasons to put time and resources into propagating your change. The first one is for the sake of the change. 'Lobbing' your change out there and hoping for the best is unlikely to give it the best chance of thriving. Those on the receiving end may not be as ready, willing or able to adopt it as you'd like and the change can quickly fall by the wayside. If it creates a negative impact elsewhere or is prevented from being embedded by other elements of the environment you won't enjoy your full benefits. The other reason for nurturing your change in the early days is for the sake of your business. Even if you are well prepared implementation of the change will uncover plenty of things no one has thought about and these will be impacting on your productivity and your people's ability to do their job. If problems aren't addressed promptly staff become demoralized and this starts to impact on your customers.

Early organizational change theory talked about unfreezing, changing and then re-freezing your organization (Lewin, 1951). It's hard to remember a time when we had the luxury of 're-freezing' and today's rate of change means we need to continually integrate one change after another into our teams. This means leaders must maintain a constant awareness of the changes impacting their teams – the lead up, implementation and embedding stages of each.

The majority of the time it is the job of line managers to propagate a new change and they can make or break it at this point. Most managers have no idea they are so critical to success so it is no surprise they are generally ill-equipped to play this role well. Organizations have spent years recruiting, training and rewarding managers who maintain the status quo – keep the ship stable at all costs. Change threatens that stability and traditional managers can inadvertently undermine the change by resisting rather than accepting the disruption it causes.

Most organizations underestimate the enormity of what we ask our change leaders to do. They expect managers to quickly overcome their own fear, uncertainty and doubt about a change so they can inform, engage and reassure their teams whilst maintaining the performance of their business. Leaders need to understand the changes, support their team members, communicate effectively, advocate for the change and reinforce it when it arrives. Without specific support we are asking the impossible of our leaders.

Although the 'propagate' step clearly ramps up after implementation, the groundwork for this phase is laid throughout the earlier stages of the cycle. Early on you'll need to know who is responsible for embedding the change so you can engage them to have their say all the way through. As part of the work to *deliver* and *prepare* for the change you will be working closely with these leaders to ensure the change is as easy as possible to adopt and embed once it is implemented. In the period immediately before the implementation you will be working with them to identify the processes for receiving and actioning feedback and the ways in which you will monitor whether the change is sticking. Once the change is implemented the real action starts. Managers of the impacted teams have the primary responsibility for making it stick and that responsibility lasts for as long as necessary to achieve the benefits.

If the *director*, *driver*, *deliverer* and *preparers* have done their job well the business should be in receipt of a change which integrates smoothly and easily. You won't truly understand the change or its impact until it is fully installed. Just as every chapter has reinforced the need to stay flexible and realign in response to new information, at this point you need to be open to what your change has or could become.

It is surprising that any organization would take their eye off the prize at this critical stage but many do. Despite evidence time and time again telling them that implementation is fraught with risks they continue to turn a blind eye a week or two after 'go-live' and long before the benefits have been sustainably delivered. With the best will in the world there will be surprises that come with change. We should expect them and be ready to deal with them.

The case study below shows the attempt by a group of line managers in a government department to increase the emphasis put on managing those post-implementation risks.

CASE STUDY   Post-implementation risks

The fines processing department had been on the receiving end of several changes over the last few months. Whilst they were reasonably well prepared for each one there was increasing frustration among the team leaders in the department about unrealistic expectations and lack of support. Every change seemed to create the same problems but the project teams never seemed to learn. A week or two after implementation the only thing they wanted to talk about was getting the post-implementation review out of the way and closing off the budgets. The department's team leaders were determined to improve the way changes were embedded in their department and so worked together with their teams to develop the 'Change Guarantee' as a way of highlighting the inevitable post-implementation events and ensuring they were taken into consideration for future changes. (See Figure 4.5.1.)

They lobbied their senior change sponsors, project management office and governance forums for months. Eventually the project methodologies and budget frameworks were adapted to include an additional phase after implementation called 'Embedding the change'. This ensured that activities and resources were planned for as long as it would take to sustainably deliver the benefits of each change and the team leaders would get the support they needed to effectively embed the changes in their teams.

Figure 4.5.1 Change guarantee

The Change Guarantee

When a change is implemented the following <u>will</u> happen and <u>will</u> require attention, action, time and resources:

1. There will be unintended consequences and ripple effects from the change that we must address.

2. Some or all of the solution will not do what *you* thought it would and you'll need to fix it.

3. Some or all of the solution will not do what *we* thought it would and we'll need to negotiate.

4. We will think of additional things we need and we'd like you to listen, consider our position and set our expectations.

5. We will be slow to get up to speed and you'll need to cut us some slack, be patient and provide additional support and training until we are more confident.

6. Our people will find ingenious ways of surreptitiously working around the bits of the change they don't understand or can't do and together we will need to build trust and a smart measurement system to help us deal with this.

Making new behaviours stick

Getting people to do things differently is always going to be hard. We are comfortable and confident with the current processes (which incidentally were new once!) which require little attention, energy or risk. New tasks take sustained effort and if we cannot or will not maintain the focus our autopilot pulls us back to the old ways or easier ways. Most organizational changes don't have life threatening consequences but even a change that will save your life can be hard to stick to. If you know someone who has had to change their lifestyle following a heart attack you'll know how hard some changes can be to make sustainably.

'More than 2.5 million baby boomers are likely to have a potentially fatal heart attack or stroke in the next five years because they refuse to lose weight, exercise or take blood pressure medication... about one in five people stopped taking blood pressure medication after a month and 80 per cent stopped after 30 months' (*Sydney Morning Herald* report on Access Economics Research, 29 November 2011).

The model made popular by Jonathan Haidt of the elephant and the rider is invaluable in understanding the inevitability or relapse in the face of major behavioural change (Heath and Heath, 2010). Based on sound psychological and neurological principles it explains how getting people to change their habits and behaviours is like a rider trying to redirect an elephant. The rider represents our rational self; analysing information, drawing conclusions and trying to align our direction to the change by pulling the elephant in the required direction. The elephant, however, represents our subconscious or autonomic self. The one with habits and urges that are hard to break. The elephant is clearly much larger than the rider, is much stronger and has more stamina. The rider may be able to redirect the elephant for a short period of time but in the long run the elephant will have his way. By way of example, it is the rider who reasons that acting as one team after a merger is the right thing to do. When that reasoning is front of mind and stress levels are low you may well act in this way, as the rider directs the elephant. A couple of weeks later when stress is high and the rider is tired the elephant takes over and you find yourself talking about 'us and them'. As Haidt suggests, find out what the elephant cares about and appeal to that; direct the rider with clear, simple instructions and shape the path so the elephant can't do a u-turn. It takes clever tactics and sustained effort to make the elephant do what you need.

Another useful framework for influencing sustainable behaviour change and creating a positive and unavoidable momentum comes from the work of Senge (1999). This outlines three reinforcing aspects which, if they are all covered in some way, create a significant force for individual change. It suggests targeting the individual's beliefs about their broader community, their team and themselves and finding links between the change and each of these to create a sustainable impetus for change. For example people will be motivated by a sense of meaning if they feel the change matters to the organization, their customers or the community. Their basic need to fit in with the tribe can be triggered if we can build a belief that the change matters to their colleagues (see the case study below). Ultimately they should also believe that they will be more successful as a result of them changing. During the transition period (where results may go down before they go up) and where a change really has no benefit for them this can be particularly tough.

'The probability of actually having the change take root is enhanced when people feel their work is challenging, when they can participate in decisions regarding how the change will be achieved, and when their interpersonal relationships are characterized by mutual trust' (Schneider, Brief and Guzzo, 1996).[26]

Your primary aim should always be for everyone to demonstrate commitment under their own steam driven by their own beliefs. Throughout the change your engagement strategy will have aimed to enlist an appropriate level of support from those impacted such that they believe in the value of the change and voluntarily comply. Realistically however you are likely to need to persuade people at least in the early stages. To do this there needs to be a compelling and meaningful consequence for changing and for not changing for each individual. Always start with an assumption of positive intent. Whilst there may be troublemakers among the team they and most other resisters during the early days are driven by fear and therefore need support more than scrutiny and punishment.

So in addition to aligning their beliefs there are three strategies that can be used to encourage them to do what you need them to do. Depending on the change, risks, culture and people involved a different mix of these is appropriate.

Carrot. Reward them for doing the right thing with something those individuals value. The sales teams may prefer a party and public praise but the IT team may prefer cinema tickets. For example, 'the sales person who gets the best client engagement scores this month gets to have lunch with the CEO'.

Stick. Inflict penalties for doing the wrong thing. Remembering that in general people are not deliberately doing the wrong thing these penalties should start with minor consequences such as the absence of rewards. For example, 'My colleague Jane won the competition for data accuracy this week. My boss is going to help me understand what I need to do to improve my score.'

Burning bridges. A strong but often neglected strategy is to make it impossible for your people to do things any other way – the equivalent of shaping the elephant's path. This means having a focus on these factors during the design of the solution. A simple example is in the embedding of a new system that automates a manual process. The design of the system and the associated processes can ensure that it is not possible to complete the transaction unless every worker uses the new system in the way it was intended. Here's what a team member may encounter when they try to work around such a system. 'Most of my customers don't have their tax details with them when they apply so we used to enter '99999' in the old system and it would let us carry on with the application. I tried putting '99999' in the new system but it's clever! It knows when I have tried to trick it and won't let me complete the application until I have entered the right information.'

Many of the changes you made to prepare your environment in the previous chapter will be great ways of burning bridges. For example, if you've taken the office walls down it's hard for managers to display hierarchical behaviours. The new open office forces ongoing interaction between managers and their teams which will be critical to changing to a more egalitarian culture. The case study below shows what one team did to embed the use of a new system in their organization.

CASE STUDY   Changing behaviours sustainably

A new workflow system was being designed to automate customer orders at a greeting card wholesaler. Line managers from the impacted teams were involved in the design and were particularly keen to ensure that as far as possible it would not be feasible for their people to work outside of the new process. They knew that one of the major changes their sales people would have to make was to improve the accuracy of the data they entered into the system. Currently the accounts team sorted out any anomalies before the clients were billed but when the new system came in the data entered at the time of order would drive distribution, stock control and accounts. If the order wasn't entered properly everything would be out of whack.

Martin the team leader had discussed this with his team as the system was being built. Data accuracy was going to be important but this had never been a strength of the team; they had always valued speed over accuracy. Now with 'go-live' only a couple of weeks away he sat down with them to work out how they would approach it. As far as possible they had designed checks into the process and system but there were still several areas where the team would need to enter information. Martin wanted to introduce a strategy that would 'catch them doing it right' rather than make them feel they were being 'checked up on' so he asked the team to develop a method that would measure the right thing and that they'd be happy with.

First, the team put up on the wall the end-to-end process which demonstrated that they were the first step and showed how the data they entered flowed through the various teams in the organization. Above it on the wall they posted the slogan 'Right First Time'. They copied this slogan onto stickers and stuck them above everyone's computer to remind them. They visited the other departments and asked them to explain the problems that inaccurate data could cause – they were considerable! At these meetings they made it clear that if any of the downstream teams found any problems with the data they were to refer it back to the sales team and not try to fix it as they had in the past.

Next they set a target. Their current data accuracy rates turned out to be a rather disappointing 67 per cent and some of the team thought that 100 per cent data accuracy was not achievable. They settled for a target of 90 per cent in the first two weeks with a plan to increase it to 100 per cent after that. Martin had anticipated that productivity would slow down while they became accustomed to the new system. He had a budget for overtime and had suspended their performance ladder for the month, replacing it with a bonus based on team performance. In the first three days they decided to check each other's data and put the percentage of accurate orders up on a chart in Martin's office.

On the first day they managed 76 per cent of the orders 'right first time'. It was clear that some team members were struggling more than others but the measure and the reward were team-based so everyone helped out. One of the team members found an online typing course with a fun test at the end which everyone used to balance their personal need for speed with the organization's need for accuracy. Martin provided extra coaching for those that needed it. It had certainly slowed down order processing but they were still on top of it and they knew it was important to get this right early. By the end of the third day their accuracy rates were up to 85 per cent so they kept the checks up till the end of the first week when they achieved 90 per cent. They knew that wasn't the end of the story though. They were pretty sure that as soon as the competition and the peer checks were no longer providing visibility and motivation they'd slip back to their old ways. After all, they'd have their sales targets to meet and the quicker you entered the orders into the system the quicker you'd be back out there selling.

To get around this they suggested that Martin do a random check and agreed to publicly sharing the individual results of this. The first person to maintain 100 per cent accuracy throughout the month would get an extra 2 per cent commission that month. As a penalty, the person with the highest rate of inaccuracy had to clean the office kitchen for a week and empty the dishwasher. They had also asked those teams downstream of them to send orders back when they weren't entered properly and this was to be avoided at all cost! It slowed the process down considerably, delayed delivery to the customer and caused frustration for the sales person. After a while it became normal for the sales people to enter their data quickly and accurately. Indeed no one even seemed to talk about it anymore.

Measuring whether the change has stuck

It is commonly quoted that 'what gets measured gets managed' and there is real evidence that measurement-managed organizations have twice the chances of success with their change programmes (Lingle and Schiemann, 1996). First, you'll need to understand what you need to stick to deliver the benefits. For example, is data accuracy important or adherence to a new process or is it behaviours and attitudes that need to change?

Next you'll need to know to what extent the change needs to stick to give you the benefits you need. Does everyone need to change or is it okay if 70 per cent of the team are doing what you need them to do. Is 'implementation' enough ie the change has 'gone live'. Or 'installation', where the new way is integrated and is being repeated by those impacted. In most cases you'll need 'realization' – the state when you are consistently getting the results and outcomes you need from the installed change. Let's take an example to see what each of these levels of integration look like. A local florist was keen to expand its business and decided to introduce a new website that would enable customers to order online. *Implementation* was achieved when the new website was available for customers to order flowers. *Installation* was achieved when existing and new customers were regularly ordering flowers through the new website. *Realization* for them was when the new ordering channel had sustainably increased the size of their customer base by > 100 per cent and their profit by > 30 per cent in the first year.

Next you'll need to decide what evidence you will look for to tell you whether the change is sticking. Is there a source of objective data or will you need to make subjective judgements? How will these measures impact on people's behaviour? If you are monitoring compliance to a new process and decide to look for evidence by observing your people – how will they react? Will they feel like they are being 'checked up on' and 'caught doing it wrong'? Will they be more or less likely to ask questions and raise concerns? How will you ameliorate this?

CASE STUDY   The wrong stickiness measures

The PFB Finance Company provide car insurance and loans via a network of car dealerships. They had just rolled out new software to the dealers to make it easier for them to offer the PFB product to their customers. The dealers had been involved in the design and after some online training the software was deployed. The project team decided to use 'number of calls to the help desk' as the measure of how well the change was sticking. They figured that when the number of calls started to drop everyone would be okay with the new system and they'd start to see revenues rise. With 200 dealers involved they decided that when they were getting fewer than 10 calls per day to the help desk about the new software the change would have stuck. In the first week of operation they had 180 calls but this quickly started to fall. By the fourth week they were delighted to see that calls had dropped to below 10 per day and they started to shut down the project.

Megan the project sponsor had agreed the number of help desk calls as the 'stickiness' indicator but she had an uneasy feeling this was not telling her the whole story. The software was supposed to increase product revenue by 20 per cent and she had seen no improvement since the software was rolled out a month ago. She rang a few dealers and they all told her that the new software was great and that it was going to make it much easier to sell the PFB product so now she was confused. Finally she decided to go and visit a dealer in her home town that she had known for a while. As soon as she walked through the door she could see something was wrong. Frank the manager seemed embarrassed to see her. 'I don't understand it Frank,' said Megan. 'Everyone loves the new software, there's hardly any calls to the help desk now so people seem to have picked it up really quickly but it's not translating into increased sales and I don't understand why.' Frank looked at her sympathetically. 'The reason no one's calling the help desk is that no one's using it but they haven't got the heart to tell you.' Over a cup of coffee Frank explained how most of the dealers he had spoken to had been looking forward to the new software and had found the training straightforward but when they tried to use it with a customer it seemed to take ages and the customers had become impatient. For the first week or so Frank and most of the other dealers had rung the help desk to see if they were doing something wrong but there didn't seem to be any quick fix. They were all busy and so opted for avoiding the software altogether and reverting to the competitor's product as their paper-based process was easier to use.

No wonder the calls to the help desk went down – most dealers were avoiding using the software after the first couple of weeks. If Megan didn't do something to fix this quickly the software would be seen as a failure, they'd have wasted their money and were in danger of putting existing revenue at risk too. When they had addressed the dealers concerns she would need to look for different evidence to see whether the change was sticking.

You can see from this case study how easy it is to get it wrong and how we can feel a false sense of security from our reporting that isn't representative of reality. By contrast the next case study shows how powerful the right measures can be to help the change stick and also to provide reliable transparency about how well it is being adopted and embedded.

CASE STUDY   The right stickiness measures

Charlesworth Accounting had taken over Davis & Associates Accountants after they encountered some financial difficulties. For Charlesworth this was a great opportunity to expand their client base, increase revenue and adopt some of the leading edge practices in use in Davis & Associates. Above all, they needed to ensure that service to the clients of both organizations was not disrupted during the merger and that staff from both organizations presented a confident, positive and united front. This was not going to be easy given the potential for a 'them and us' culture between staff from each entity.

The change management programme worked with business leaders from both entities to prepare people for the changes. As part of this programme they ran workshops with people from both organizations asking them to identify the needs of the customers during the transition. When the output from these workshops was collated the list was presented to the managing director.

Figure 4.5.2   Client outcomes

> **Our clients want ...**
> 1. To feel positive about the merger
> 2. Us to be loyal to our organization
> 3. Us to be confident about service levels during transition
> 4. The merger to bring them benefits

Frances, the managing director, was sure that if the clients' needs were met Charlesworth would achieve the benefits it needed in return for its investment in Davis. She hoped that a strong focus on the client would be a good way of bonding the employees from both organizations to a common goal and distracting them from creating destructive factions. A thorough leadership, communications, training and support programme was established to help everyone deal effectively with their clients.

When it came to deciding what measures they would use to ensure the change was sticking they decided to use the same four criteria and designed a simple client questionnaire which everyone would ask their clients to complete at the end of client meetings in the first few months of the merger (Figure 4.5.3). Importantly, allowance was made for those clients who already had a difficult relationship with either company. Anyone whose clients gave poor feedback would be offered additional help to enable them to improve the results.

After discussions with the staff they settled on a target of > 80 per cent of clients answering 'agree' or 'strongly agree' to at least three of the questions for three consecutive months. As the report in Figure 4.5.4 shows, after six months that target was finally met.

It turned out Frances had been right: a calm and contented client base was resulting in stronger revenue streams and people from both organizations had worked hard to share knowledge and streamline processes behind the scenes in order to lift these scores.

Figure 4.5.3   Client survey

Charlesworth / Davis Post Merger Client Feedback

	Strongly Disagree	Disagree	Agree	Strongly Agree
1. I feel positively about the merger	☐	☐	☐	☐
2. I believe your people are loyal to their organization	☐	☐	☐	☐
3. I am confident that service levels will be maintained during the transition	☐			
4. The merger will benefit me in some way				

Thank you

Frances Cl

Figure 4.5.4   'Stickiness' report

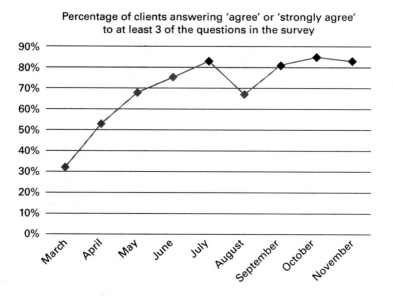

Percentage of clients answering 'agree' or 'strongly agree' to at least 3 of the questions in the survey

---

Think ...

1   Do leaders in our organization understand that they are accountable for making changes stick so that benefits can be realized?

_____

_____

_____

2   The evidence we will look for to tell us whether the change is sticking in the right way is...

_____

_____

_____

Propagate traps

It's easy to see how some of the traps outlined in previous chapters can undermine this critical stage of the change. For example having project rather than business leaders *drive* the change; removing all resources and governance a week or two after *delivery*; or failing to *prepare* the people who will be given guardianship of this fragile change. Let's look at some of the other views and activities that could be holding you back from effectively propagating your change.

Trap 1: Our people are 'change fatigued'

It may be a great change but they are so tired of change they can't put in the effort they need to adopt this one. There has been an increasing trend in recent years towards a feeling among managers and their teams of being overwhelmed by changes. Whilst this may reflect the increasing rate and complexity of organizational changes, it is also exacerbated by poor organizational change management. The phrase 'change fatigue' is too often used by leaders as an excuse for poor change design, inadequate preparation, badly timed and executed implementation and insufficient support. Your people may not be tired of change – they may be tired of bad change.

Trap 2: We are not ready

We thought we had enough skills and commitment to launch the change. We thought we had addressed as many of their concerns as was realistic. Everyone was behaving as if they were looking forward to the change but now it's here they are complaining and saying they need more training. Equally we tried to make sure we prepared the environment so that nothing conflicted with our change but we hadn't bargained on a change to the finance policy coming into force at the same time and fundamentally undermining the empowered mindset we need for our change to succeed. Whether we could or couldn't have prepared better is not a useful discussion once the change has gone live. As the team leaders in the government call centre were keen to remind the project teams in the earlier case study – you *will* find surprises so expect them and be ready to deal with them.

Trap 3: 'You never told me...'

No matter how thorough your communications campaign there will always be people who chose not to attend the briefings, read the e-mails or complete the training. If this avoidance is driven by fear these people will be the first to offer a range of seemingly plausible reasons why they cannot adopt the change. Even if these concerns are not based on fact they will still claim that changes to scope weren't communicated, insufficient training was offered or a problem with a small part of the new system means that the whole change has to be reversed. Inwardly they are panicking and will be lobbying for others to join their cause. If these people are influential in the team they can have a considerable negative effect in the important early days of a change.

Trap 4: We don't plan the transition

Sometimes we have the perfect solution ready for *delivery* and a perfectly *prepared* environment but we don't put sufficient attention into the transition of one into the other. As a result we are not clear about roles, timelines, fallback plans, escalation and decision-making procedures. The inevitable transition risks turn to obstacles and the implementation becomes troublesome. It's not clear whose problem it is, everyone gets frustrated and withdraws their co-operation. A perfectly good change is tainted and loses critical support because of the way it was implemented.

Trap 5: No one is watching

There could be many reasons for this. Perhaps our managers don't know they have a role to play or are too busy. Perhaps we believe the change is finished once it is implemented and we have already moved on to the next big thing. People do what they believe their bosses think is important so if the leaders are not ready, willing and able to visibly reinforce the change it will not stick.

Trap 6: We don't measure 'embeddedness'

For some changes we just don't think about it and as a result we have no idea of the level or type of adoption we require to deliver our benefits. As a consequence we never discuss how we will measure whether the change has stuck and have no criteria or targets to work to. When we do have targets it can be difficult to decide what evidence is appropriate, valid, reasonably available, and will reinforce the culture and behaviours the change needs. Couple this with the time, resources, transparency and accountability involved in measuring the change and it's easy to see how tempting it can be to declare the change a success (regardless of the evidence!) and move on.

Trap 7: We run out of money

Our budget covered the design and delivery of the solution and the work needed to get the people and the environment ready for change. Now the change is live it turns out we need to do some coaching to bolster the team's skill levels. In addition, the sales team have implemented a work-around for a problem that no one had thought of. That workaround means some of the data is now outside of the new system and their workload has increased by 20 per cent. They just need a couple of small changes to the system to sort it out... but you've got no money. There's no budget set aside for this post-implementation phase so the development team have already moved on and the business will just have to find the people and funding to fix the problems!

Trap 8: Humans will be humans!

Inevitably some of our people will spend inordinate amounts of energy trying to rebuild the old ways and work around the new ways. We can be very resourceful (or crafty) when it comes to avoiding something we don't want to do. After all it is human nature to find the quickest and easiest way to get the outcome we need. Where the 'right way' just seems too hard we will break whatever rules we need to in order to get what we need more easily. Depending on the prevailing culture these workarounds may be public or they may be kept secret. Before we know it our change is undermined, unhelpful behaviours have set in and we'll need to work hard to get our change back on track.

Consider a 'no parking' zone outside the supermarket. When there are other spaces not far away we make the extra effort and comply with the 'No Parking' zone. But when the only available spaces are right at the back of the car park we'll weigh up our chances of getting caught versus the convenience of that spot in front of the door. If we park in the 'No Parking' zone a few times and don't get caught we are likely to park there every time and no longer see this as the 'wrong' thing to do. The same logic applies when we are asked to change at work. New tasks are naturally hard – we've never done them before. If we can find an easier way and we won't get caught we'll take it. If we fear getting caught we will go to great lengths to fake compliance and cover up our workarounds.

Trap 9: We resist accountability

Openly measuring and reporting on elements of our business performance brings with it a level of transparency and accountability that may make us uncomfortable. As individuals we have a natural aversion to holding ourselves up for scrutiny. Within our organization historical and cultural factors may lead us to fear singular accountability. For example, if our organization always looks for someone to blame when things go wrong we will be extremely reluctant to take that risk. Either way – if we don't put these measures in place and use them as a lever for change the potential for our change to unravel is significant.

Trap 10: We expect to return to 'business as usual' after the change

In fact business should not be 'as usual' or the change has failed – the business should be different. In response to a desperate need to get back in control we try to lock down the inevitable turbulence that change creates before we are confident that it is working in the way we need it to. For example, we overlook some of the teething troubles in the interests of stability and certainty. We turn a blind eye to the impact of the workarounds so we can all 'get back to normal'. We may be storing up problems for later and we are almost certainly undermining the success of our change but it is making us feel better now.

> **Think...**
>
> 1   Which of these traps is holding back your change?
>
> 2   Which one, if you fixed it, would bring the greatest benefit?

Propagate tips

So now you have identified some of the things that may be holding you back let's look at some ideas to help your change to stick to the extent you need to deliver the benefits.

Idea 1: Recruit, train and reward change leadership

Don't wait until your organization has a change it wants to embed before building change leadership capability in your managers. Provide support for them to understand the different role they need to play during change and build the competence to handle the challenges change presents. They will need to be able to manage their own reactions to change quickly and effectively, manage their team members' reactions and have skills and knowledge to effectively understand, support, communicate, advocate and reinforce change.

> Most organizations underestimate the enormity of what we ask our change leaders to do.

Idea 2: Expect people to relapse and plan for it

Both the people and the environment will resist the change in the early days. No matter how ready you thought you were it is inevitable. Rather than get caught out try to anticipate the areas that might trip you up and plan for ways to mitigate their effect. Just before you implement the change the change manager will do a 'readiness assessment'. Whilst you hope this confirms that everything is ready to go, it will inevitably contain valuable insights into the likely post-implementation problems and you should get working on these as soon as you have the information. Just as importantly, once the change has been implemented be ready to find and deal with things you hadn't expected. Having effective feedback channels, monitoring mechanisms, management forums (made up of both 'deliverers' and 'receivers'), processes and resources in place to act on problems quickly and effectively sends a strong message about how important embedding the change, and therefore delivering the benefits, is.

Idea 3: Ensure the 'receivers' have their say

There are two phases of a project where the people on the receiving end of the change should have considerable influence. As we've seen one of these is the design phase when elements of the solution can be designed to make embedding the change easier for example by finding ways to 'burn bridges', avoid workarounds and ensuring compliance is 'locked in'. People receiving the change must also have significant influence over the timing and method of implementation. They will not be able to give the change the attention it needs if they feel ambushed by it or overwhelmed with the confusion and exhaustion caused by multiple, incompatible changes hitting them all at the same time. The Hammonds Change Calendar in Chapter 3.2 showed how the shop managers had a seat at the table where they could influence the timing and way in which changes were introduced. It may suit the delivery team to go live with a new system 'big bang' all on one day but if the business cannot absorb that impact they need to find a better way.

Idea 4: Plan to make it better

Add time, money and resources to reinforce changes through further training, communication or development activity. Provide an improvement path following implementation of the change. Train people to higher levels of competence to enable you to realize even greater benefits. As the pace of change increases in our organizations – each bringing their own revelations – the case for a more 'agile' approach to change strengthens. It is easy to see how rolling out small changes more often builds the expectation and ability to deliver changes, and therefore benefits, earlier and refine them *in situ*.

Idea 5: Use measurement as a lever for change

You'll need some data or evidence to tell you whether the change is sticking in the way you need it to but you know that what you measure and the way you measure it will have a significant effect on the way your people react to the change. Work with impacted people and their managers to identify what evidence to look for, the targets to set and how to report it. Focus on no more than three measures that each has a clear link to the desired outcome, minimal negative impact on behaviours and for which the data is relatively easy to collect. This involvement of the people who will ultimately be measured has the added benefit of reinforcing the desired outcome and giving them an increased sense of control and ownership. When the measures are in place make it matter with positive and negative consequences as appropriate for your team. Above all measure in a way that targets the right signals and maintains open communication channels. Constantly challenge those results against anecdotal evidence to make sure you are interpreting the signs correctly. The tool is Appendix 10 will help you plan your approach to measuring and reporting during this phase.

Criteria for change 'stickiness' measures

- no more than three measures;
- each has a clear link to the desired outcome;
- minimal negative impact on behaviours;
- data is relatively easy to collect.

Idea 6: Workarounds are your friend

Create an environment where the people impacted are comfortable raising and discussing the workarounds they feel are necessary or desirable. We all want to make our lives easier and if someone has found a way of speeding things up we want to hear about it. On the positive side an open discussion about workarounds has the potential to uncover simple but effective improvements that everyone can benefit from and problems with the solution that need to be addressed. As a strategy to help embed the change the discussion enables the people impacted to realize the problems their workaround will cause others and therefore comply with the new process.

Idea 7: Don't take your eye off the ball

Whilst not all of your people will be focused on undermining your change some will and they will be looking for any opportunity to go back to their old ways. Like the child that doesn't want to stay in bed at night, the moment you turn your back, they are creeping back down the stairs. The moment you look as if you have turned your attention to something else those still reticent about the change will go back to their old ways or develop destructive workarounds.

Idea 8: Keep burning their bridges

If you absolutely need people to follow a new process or use a system in a certain way to get your benefits, then as far as possible take away the opportunity to do something different. Assuming you've done all you can in the design of the solution once it is implemented you need to be vigilant to the new bridges your people are building back to the old ways or easier ways. Change leaders must intercept quickly and burn the new bridge in a way that demonstrates to others that bridge-building back to the old ways is futile. The challenge for the change leader is to keep burning those bridges whilst institutionalizing the new behaviours.

Idea 9: Provide LOTS of support for your managers

Middle managers will be the biggest handbrake or the most powerful accelerator for your change. In the early days after implementation line managers can make or break a change. Their role is a tough one; trying to run their business, manage their own reaction and that of their team as well as deal with inevitable teething troubles. The scrutiny of the change measures may be adding to their woes. As these people are the most important lever for change at this point treat them like it. Make sure their voices are heard and problems are addressed quickly. Empower them to make decisions that will help the change succeed and provide them with the coaching support they need to manage the emotional as well as the business impact on them and their teams.

Idea 10: Create an unavoidable momentum to change

If you are lucky your change is so popular that it develops a momentum of its own. For example, if it solves a tiresome problem, is easy to adopt and everyone around you seems to have adopted it then you are likely to go with the flow. Even if your change is not that popular if you are maintaining the focus in the weeks and months after it is introduced, continuing to reinforce the vision, are quick to respond to attempts to derail it and celebrating achievements, it is possible to create an unavoidable groundswell of support.

Think...

1 Which of these ideas could help your organization?

2 Which one would give you the most benefit?

So...

When you know which *direction* you need to go in, have a confident and competent *driver*, the right solution is ready to *deliver* and you've *prepared* your people and the environment your change is looking in good shape. But you are only two thirds of the way through the change cycle so what happens next? The tool in Appendix 10 provides a process to help you plan how to measure whether your change is being embedded, what data to collect and how it will be reported. In the meantime, the questions below will get you thinking about areas you may need to address to improve the way you propagate change.

1   What is likely to get in the way of our change sticking in the way we need in order to realize our benefits?

_____

_____

_____

_____

2   What can be done as part of the design of the change to burn their bridges back to the old ways?

_____

_____

_____

_____

3   Does the evidence suggest that we allocate sufficient money and time after implementation to refine and embed changes and build confidence? If not, what do we need to do more of, less of, start doing or stop doing?

_____

_____

_____

_____

4   Does the evidence suggest our impacted leaders have the knowledge and skill to be able to effectively adopt and embed new changes (ie to understand, support, communicate, advocate and reinforce the change)? If not, which gaps do we need to address first?

_____

_____

_____

_____

5 Do we measure and report on whether your change has stuck?

If not, what simple measures could we introduce to check whether our next change is being adopted and embedded? Who should we involve in this decision?

_____

_____

_____

_____

If we do, do we measure and report in a way that encourages open communication and constructive behaviour among those impacted?

_____

_____

_____

_____

6 The most important thing I need to remember about propagating change is ...

_____

_____

_____

_____

Want to know more?

Search engine terms: embedding change, behaviour change, sustainable change, reactions to change, change leadership.

Profit from the change

Profit: to gain an advantage or benefit

Successful organizations profit from their changes by fully realizing the benefits they need.

Figure 4.6   Profit from the change

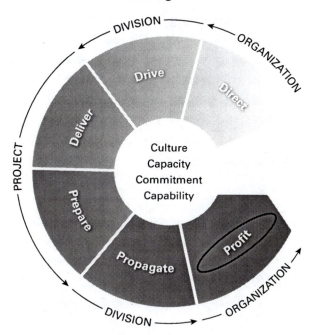

Successful organizations *profit* from their changes. They set achievable benefit goals, keep an eye on them and celebrate their delivery. Benefits are clearly articulated, easily measured and remain visible throughout the change. They underpin the vision, are fundamental to strategy decisions, change programme governance and decision making. The change comes full circle as it delivers the *direction* that was set and in turn updates the organization's roadmap of change.

'$45bn... investment in IT... has not produced measureable gains' (Booz Allen Hamilton, 2002).

'60 per cent of CFOs find their IT investments are not producing the returns they expected' (*CFO Magazine* survey, 2005).[27]

'86 per cent of projects reported losing up to 25 per cent of expected benefits' (KPMG, 2005).

'61 per cent of takeovers and mergers destroy shareholder value' (Henry and Jespersen, 2002).

The fundamental reason for embarking on a change is to realize a benefit but if you look at those odds you will see that if you invest in change in most organizations you have about a one in three chance of realizing the return you need. Would you give them your own money at these odds? You'd be better off betting on the horses! Yet organizations continue to speculate with large amounts of shareholder, taxpayer or donor money every year. We see the potential for a disastrous return on investment and yet you can be sure that most of these organizations are still rolling out changes in largely the same way!

In a study of over 1,500 projects, 84 per cent of the project managers did not think the benefits for their project would be realized by the business while around 50 per cent of the impacted business representatives held that view (Tranzform Group, 2009).

Benefits

A benefit is a business outcome that delivers value to the organization. Benefits are the beginning, middle and end of the change story. You need them badly enough to invest time, money and energy to get them; you care about them enough to make sure you are on track to achieve them; and when the change is in, you make sure you get them. The success of your benefits realization is the primary indicator of the success of your investment. This book has frequently used the phrase 'successful change' and whilst you may have your own view of what this means, a change is successful in the eyes of the organization and its shareholders only if it works sufficiently, appropriately and sustainably to realize the new state your organization needs in return for a reasonable level of investment.[28]

Benefits can be anything your organization needs and are commonly articulated in terms of something being quicker, cheaper or better. Examples include an increase in productivity, increased revenue, cost reduction, greater market share, regulatory compliance, increased customer satisfaction or reduction in staff turnover. The value a benefit delivers can be direct or indirect. For example, a company may build an outdoor learning area at a local school and clearly the children and the school will benefit directly from this. Indirectly, however, the organization will see their return on investment coming from increased revenue through the greater brand loyalty they hope this change will engender in the parents.

Not all benefits are of equal importance. Depending on the strategic objective you are trying to meet some benefits will make a greater contribution than others and they will need to be prioritized. The strategic objective itself sits within a series of organizational priorities and this will influence the way you monitor and manage the associated benefits.

As we've seen, delivery of the change is not the same as delivery of the benefits and very few changes deliver their benefits on or before Day One. Equally it doesn't necessarily follow that because the change has been delivered the benefits will be achieved automatically yet these views still seem to be behind the approach a lot of organizations take. Figure 4.6.1 illustrates how the delivery of the change starts the post-implementation benefits realization process. It also shows the steps that link change delivery with benefits realization and a more successful organization.

To break this down into a useful framework Figure 4.6.2 shows the interim steps that need to happen between project delivery and benefits realization. It shows how the change that is delivered first needs to be embedded to the extent that it creates the *change outcome* that was anticipated. It then shows how this change outcome is applied to the day-to-day business to achieve the specific *business outcome* the organization needs to deliver all or part of its strategic objective.

Figure 4.6.1   The benefits trail

Figure 4.6.2   Path from change delivery to a more successful organization

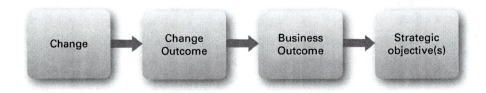

Figure 4.6.3   Path from an acquisition to benefits realization

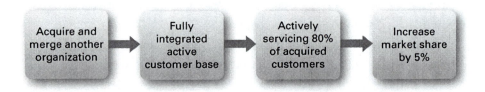

Lets look at our earlier example of the takeover by Charlesworth Accounting of Davis & Associates to see how this framework is applied. Figure 4.6.3 shows how acquiring and merging another company (the change) enabled them to have a fully integrated customer base (the change outcome) which in turn enabled the business to reach its target of actively servicing 80 per cent of the acquired customers (the business outcome) which in turn helped the organization achieve an increase in market share (strategic objective).

In another example the path from the introduction of a new bank loan workflow system to a more successful organization would look something like the flow in Figure 4.6.4.

Figure 4.6.4   The benefits trail from a new bank loan workflow system

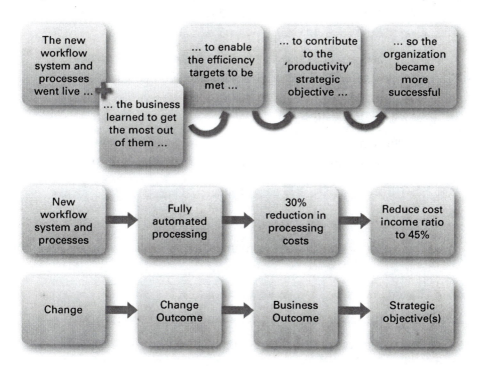

Predicting success

Often benefits related to large change programmes can seem distant and too intangible to understand or measure. In these cases it is useful to articulate the intermediate steps that will indicate the project is on the right track to deliver the benefits. Further expanding on the example of the bank with the new workflow system, the intermediate benefit indicators may look something like the following.

The **strategic objective** is to reduce the cost income ratio to 45 per cent. One of the **business outcomes** required to support the achievement of this objective is to reduce processing costs by 30 per cent. Interim **indicators before the change** is implemented could be:

- Feasibility studies indicate that the conceptual approach will address the underlying business problem and deliver the cost reduction required (so we are confident to invest more time and money).

- Processing time and costs are defined and base-lined (so we know where our starting point is).

- Business scenario modelling of the solution *design* demonstrates achievement of 30 per cent cost reduction (so we are confident we have the right solution to meet our goal).

- Interim checks during the *build* phase continue to demonstrate achievement of 30 per cent cost reduction (so we know that whatever changes have been made along the way the overall goal is still achievable).

- Solution *testing* demonstrates achievement of 30 per cent cost reduction (so we can confidently plan to realize the benefits).

Interim **indicators during the transition** would include:

- The solution is ready to deliver.

- The business people and environment are ready to receive the solution.

- The solution is working as intended.

- People are using the system in the way it was intended.

- People are confident in their use of the new system and processes.

Indicators after implementation become more focused on tangible delivery of the change outcome and the business outcome. They would also incorporate the measures we used in Chapter 4.5 to monitor the extent to which the change has stuck. For this example these may be:

- End-to-end processing time is reduced by 25 per cent on average per application.

- Improved reporting is enabling optimized resource management.

- Headcount savings are realized.

- No more paper processing.

Managing benefits

As soon as there is some direction you can define what you need to achieve – usually as part of a feasibility study, terms of reference or business case. As the change progresses, benefits remain 'front and centre' of all activities.

They are visible so that the link between them and the solution is clear. They are measured and actively reviewed throughout to ensure they remain desirable and achievable. It should go without saying but this constant focus will require you to allocate sufficient resources to the task from the very beginning to the very end. The list below outlines the focus on benefits in each component of the change cycle:

- DIRECT the change: Identify, articulate, agree, realign and reintegrate benefits.

- DRIVE the change: Build awareness and understanding of benefits and use them visibly as criteria for decision making and to energize the vision for the change.

- DELIVER the change: Measure, monitor and refine benefits.

- PREPARE for the change: Enable the 'change outcome'. Build commitment through awareness and understanding of path from change to benefits. Monitor, refine and embed ownership of benefits post-implementation.

- PROPAGATE the change: Assume responsibility for achieving the 'change outcome' and the 'business outcome'. Measure, monitor and achieve benefits.

The nature of your environment will impact on your ability to profit from change. Effective benefits management is dependent on clear ownership, accountable leaders and adequate governance. The internal and external culture has a strong influence when it comes to managing benefits. A culture that encourages transparency of business performance, a tolerance for experimentation and rewards a long-term view will provide a supportive environment where the delivery of valuable outcomes is possible. If on the other hand your organization has inconsistent processes, rewards telling people what they want to hear over the truth, punishes failure or values a short-term view then this part of the change cycle is going to be tough.

The size of the organization will also have an impact on your willingness and ability to manage benefits effectively and it is interesting to note the difference in attitude between small and large organizations. Smaller organizations have more at stake. The consequences of not getting a real return on their investment could mean the end of the organization. Large corporations seem to feel remote from their shareholders or maybe feel that the day-today business provides the returns they need and which the market values. Most take a remarkably lax approach to ensuring there actually *is* a return on their capital investment – investing millions with no way of knowing if or when they have delivered a real return.

The operating environment or industry can also have an impact on the level of diligence that return on investment naturally attracts. In general, the more public scrutiny people feel they are under the more diligent they will be about ensuring a valuable return on their investment in change. For example, not-for-profit organizations are acutely aware of their duty to their donors and the people in them are generally more driven to ensure they can articulate the outcomes they are achieving.

> Effective benefits management is dependent on clear ownership, accountable leaders and adequate governance.

Being able to reliably deliver benefits however is mainly dependent on a fully functioning change cycle with everyone contributing effectively. Across the organization there must be a strong and up-to-date roadmap of change to provide clear *direction* and the 'pull' for true benefit realization. The business units impacted by the changes must *drive* and *propagate* the change and the project teams must effectively *deliver* and *prepare* people for it. It's easy to see how if just one element of this cycle is underperforming the benefits will be in jeopardy.

Many people are involved in the identification, monitoring and realization of benefits. The most important is the benefit owner. Benefits, and the processes to support their achievement, should be owned by the senior leader with accountability for the strategic objective(s) your change is designed to support. This may be the *driver* or someone else. The benefit owner must have the power to influence the way benefits are managed and have a seat at the table when trade-off decisions are made.

While the project is active the project management office (PMO) is usually responsible for gathering the right data to be able to produce reliable reporting to support business decision making. When trade-off decisions are made which result in alterations to the scope or timing of the changes the PMO provides the frameworks and processes to quickly realign project activity accordingly.

The organization's strategy team or change management office (CMO) provides the up-to-date roadmap of change for the organization and ensures the right benefits are planned to deliver each of the strategic objectives. They are heavily involved in trade-off decisions by helping those responsible to understand the broader implications of changes to the scope, nature or timing of planned benefits.

The project manager needs a clear view of the outcomes the solution must deliver as well as the interim steps that will indicate whether the project is on track to deliver them. This information will be used throughout the project to guide priorities. The project manager is also the source of the data that is used by business leaders to track the progress of their strategic plan and are required to provide benefits forecast reporting via the PMO as part of the governance of their project.

The change manager uses the benefits, their measures and targets to develop a compelling vision for the change. They will constantly refer to the benefits and the intermediate steps to build and maintain the understanding and commitment of those involved and impacted.

The finance department is involved but supports not drives the process. Its support for benefits-related decision making is critical and operates at both strategic and a tactical level. Strategically it provides insights into investment options and capital and operating budget implications. Tactically it uses information about benefits to plan, allocate, release and realign operating and capital budgets within each change and across the organization.

Representatives from the people impacted by the change must also have input throughout the benefits cycle. In parallel with the understanding and commitment this involvement brings, they are in the best position to identify appropriate intermediate outcomes; ensure measurement data is easy to collect and reliable; take baseline measurements and decide if targets are achievable. As the change progresses, they are ideally placed to spot the early indicators of benefit failure.

Accurately identifying, tracking and revising benefits involves a wide range of people including representatives from technology, human resources and a good cross-section of business people. If your change will impact people outside of the organization they need to be represented in this activity too.

Benefits management maturity

Just as other capability within an organization grows in maturity so does benefits management. The more experience an organization has the better its processes and systems become. Figure 4.6.5 shows the evidence to look for to find out how mature your organization's approach is.

If you didn't score too well you are in good company – the majority of organizations unfortunately still have poor handover processes and protocols and no reliable way of tracking, reporting on and updating benefit projections.

Benefits management process

Figure 4.6.6 overleaf shows the four phases of benefits management from identifying and articulating them at the outset, through constant monitoring, measurement and management to realizing and rewarding them at the end and reintegrating the achievements into the organization's roadmap of change.

Identify and articulate

The first step in the process is to identify the benefits you need and articulate them in a way that is consistently understood by everyone involved. There can be a strong temptation to articulate benefits based on what you think the project will deliver rather than what the business needs. The easiest way to identify benefits is to work back from the strategic objective the change is designed to support. For example, if the strategic objective is to increase market share by 5 per cent over the next two years – what contribution does your change need to make to that objective?

For each benefit and its interim goals develop an appropriate way of measuring progress and achievement and set the relevant targets. Where possible use an existing business measure. Not only will the data collection and reporting already be established but the business will already have a process and a forum for addressing the content. Benefits measures should:

- be few in number (ideally no more than three for each benefit);
- be agreed by everyone involved as an accurate indicator of the change outcome, business outcome or benefit;
- be easy to collect reliable data;

Figure 4.6.5 Benefits Management Maturity Level Indicators

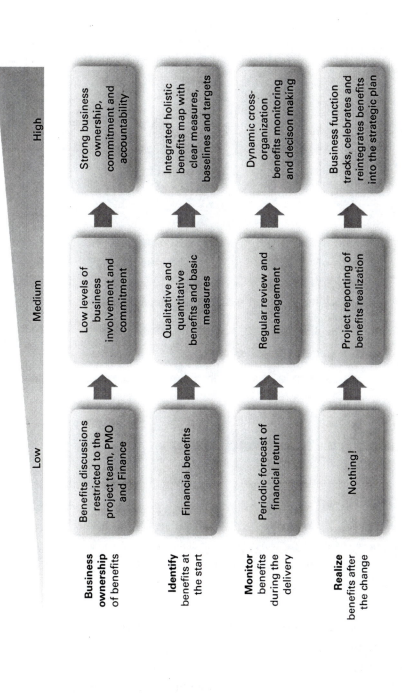

Figure 4.6.6   Benefits lifecycle

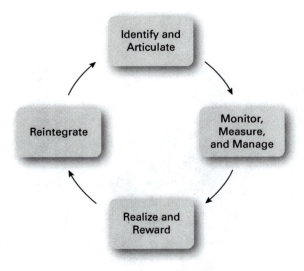

- demonstrate a clear link between the solution, the change outcome, the business outcome and the strategic objective;
- be constantly reviewed for relevance and updated as necessary;
- be reported against regularly;
- be actively and regularly discussed and acted upon by business and project leaders.

Monitor report and realign

> A completed project represents *potential* business benefits, not bankable benefits... but identifying and quantifying benefits are not enough. Unless business unit executives commit to achieving them – and have the tools to measure them – realizing the benefits is unlikely (Tucker, 2004).

As we've already seen the drivers for your change, the organizational environment strategy and targets will continually change so the benefits outlined in the business case are unlikely to remain current for long. Effective *direction*, *drive* and *delivery* will ensure new information is actively considered and that decisions are made with reference to the benefits. In parallel with this there should also be an active review by representatives from the business of their continued relevance and priority. Most project methodologies now include some form of benefits realization plan and reporting. It is often tempting to leave it up to the delivery team to provide this data but the real value can be gained from these tools when they are owned and managed by those responsible for realizing the benefits.

Figure 4.6.7 shows an extract from the benefits log in the period just before the new workflow system in the earlier example was implemented. You can see how it uses the interim outcomes linked to the benefits. This type of information is useful to the business when making decisions about if or when to implement the change and how to allocate valuable time, money and resources.

Realize

If the groundwork has been done, realizing the benefits you need is a realistic goal. By maintaining the energy through the later phases of the change and adapting the measurements to focus on the desired outcomes it is possible to complete the full cycle of change in a way that not only delivers its specific value but also equips the organization to change more successfully in the future. At this stage, the organization level of change management needs to step back in. The people who delivered the change will move on; those on the receiving end may no longer see it as a change as it becomes 'the new normal' and their attention turns to other priorities. The organization that keeps a strong and relentless focus on tracking the realization of benefits across all change programmes sends a strong message to its people and stakeholders about the importance of realizing real advantage from change.

Reintegrate

The original purpose of your change was to make a valid contribution to the overall success of the organization. As a result of your efforts you have changed the organization in some way and others now need to know that your changes are part of the new landscape they are operating in. What you have achieved or not achieved may present opportunities or obstacles for others so those benefits must now be reintegrated into the strategic road-map of change for the organization. The updated roadmap then provides the *direction* which helps other changes stay on track.

Figure 4.6.7 Example benefits log

Strategic objective	Improve productivity: reduce the cost income ratio to 45%						
Business outcome	Meet efficiency targets: reduce processing costs by 30%						
Change outcome	Owner	Measure	Planned	Forecast	Variance	This is because...	This is what we are doing about it...
Team members are confidently using the new system	Tony Smithers	Number of people who agree or strongly agree they are confident	80%	65%	–15%	The people who were trained more than 2 weeks ago are proving to be the least confident	Organizing refresher sessions for anyone that wants them. Also setting up a 'drop in' desk where people can practise and ask questions
Solution testing demonstrates achievement of 30% cost reduction	Jenny Durrant	End to end costing of six selected scenarios	30%	20%	–10%	Bugs within the accounts module are forcing a manual workaround until this is fixed	Working with the vendor to fix and re-test the module before we go live. Back-up plan is to use the workaround until a fix is found

It is at this stage, too, that there is a very public acknowledgement and celebration of the delivery of true benefit to the organization. This approach provides a constant reinforcement of the purpose and value of benefits management and change in general and is also an opportunity to communicate relevant updates to strategic plans.

Think ...

1 Is there a visible and accountable owner for benefits realization? If not what changes can we make to ensure the right person is accountable?

_____

_____

_____

2 Have we identified and articulated a full range of change outcomes, business outcomes and benefits which are consistently understood by everyone involved?

_____

_____

_____

Profit traps

If you've worked hard throughout the change it seems a shame not to know whether or to what extent you have delivered real value to the organization. Let's look at what may be stopping you from confidently answering questions about how your change has benefited the organization.

Trap 1: Ownership

Maybe we have no benefits owner or too many owners. Perhaps our owner is not displaying the level of commitment we need. They may not understand the role or have the experience and skills to perform it well. Sometimes they come in too late or stop too early. They may know something you don't about how this accountability could backfire on them. Remember poor Tom at the whitegoods company in Chapter 4.2 who had the forecast $2 million benefits taken out his budget without any understanding of how that figure would be delivered. Whatever the issue we don't know who to talk to about benefits let alone manage them.

Trap 2: Invisible forces

Understandably we have a fear of being held visibly accountable for something that appears to be out of our control. If we feel we are being set up to fail we will avoid any situation where we are individually in the spotlight to deliver something important. Whilst this is a natural human response this view will be further reinforced if it is the norm in our organization to remove all the safety nets and publicly vilify those that don't deliver. If the horror stories told around our organization talk about the poor person for whom being accountable for something that failed ruined their career we are unlikely to want to be next in their shoes.

Perhaps our culture rewards short-term success over long-term gain. Whilst the figures may demonstrate a return on investment over a period of years, the culture of our organization may be sending a different, more powerful message. If we see signals which imply we should 'deliver and move on' then beware: who is going to prepare for, propagate and ensure you profit from that change?

Trap 3: We are not walking the talk

We talk about benefits and imply that realizing them is a top priority but our actions don't support the words and the processes and systems needed to support them are not in place. Perhaps our business case process offers only limited support for effective identification and measurement of benefits. Maybe we haven't invested in tools to monitor and report on them. Often our governance processes are too slow to respond to critical information and when our benefits are in jeopardy our actions don't imply a sense of urgency. Many of our organizations stop the finance and the focus soon after implementation. All of these send a strong signal to those delivering and impacted by this change and subsequent ones that change delivery is more important than business benefits realization.

Trap 4: Some pieces of our jigsaw are missing

We start by looking for some strong organizational strategic objectives to begin the identification and articulation of our benefits. If our organization doesn't have a clear vision and strategy we could fall at this first hurdle. We find that attempts to create an anchor for our change feel somewhat unstable in the absence of an organization-wide goal.

If we can find the appropriate strategic hook for our change next we look for the list of initiatives that are designed to meet that strategic objective so that we can agree the boundaries and interdependencies between each of our changes and their benefits. If it is not clear which initiatives contribute to which strategic objective the scope and benefits of your programme are likely to remain unclear, making effective benefits management difficult.

Let's assume we have a strong strategic objective and are clear about the benefits we need to deliver. Next we look for the evidence we will need to confirm that the benefits have been realized – the business outcomes. Often all we can find is a list of what the change will deliver, for example a new structure, culture, product or system. There is a gaping hole between this and the desired benefits and we can't see how we get from one to the other.

Trap 5: We rely on the original business case

Research has shown that business cases are generally viewed only as documents for gaining funding. Once they are approved they are put away and few organizations track the business benefits projects actually achieve (Tucker, 2004). Any benefits articulated in the initial business case have three fundamental flaws. Firstly, they are estimates based on very little information – in any other area of our lives that's a guess! Secondly, they often focus primarily on financial return therefore missing the opportunity to understand the true outcome needed from the change and focusing energy and resources on this one aspect to the detriment of other, possibly more valuable outcomes. Finally, the governance structures, frameworks and processes never require this business case to be revisited.

Realistically, as we have access to more detailed planning information and can refine the objectives, scope and cost of the project, the benefits are almost certainly out of date. Again, our human nature is having an influence as we are susceptible to a concept called 'anchoring and insufficient adjustment' which explains that when faced with uncertainty humans anchor on a specific outcome or value and don't change this in the face of new information which calls it into doubt. This can be a big problem when it comes to estimating, monitoring and delivering the benefits of change. We connect firmly to an initial figure and systematically ignore any new information which may indicate a need to change it. This starts the process of making the benefits irrelevant.

Trap 6: There's no clear link

As we've seen, the power of a well-articulated benefit is in the way it flows out to the organization's objective and back to the specifics of what is being delivered. Assuming all the components are available we sometimes fail to check they make a coherent story to those who need to be informed and inspired by it. It may be that we have failed to articulate each step clearly or our statements are too vague and don't go to the lengths required to tell the end-to-end story. When this logic is not clear people get confused and inertia sets in.

Trap 7: We don't know who is looking after our benefits

When there is a significant focus on the design and build of the change we may not invest sufficient time in engaging the right people and processes to look after our benefits. If it is not clear who the owner is, who needs to be involved, who is tracking and reporting progress and making the decisions it is likely our benefits will go by the wayside and managing them will become an afterthought. If the benefit owner is not consulted up front and involved throughout you will have lost a key lever for the sustainability of your change.

Trap 8: We don't know how we are measuring success

To get us through the business case we needed to identify the benefits we would deliver in return for the investment in our change. We weren't asked how we would measure them and as a result we are well into our change and we don't have any idea of our starting point or how we will measure whether we are on track to deliver our benefits. Often it feels too hard to develop or agree to the right measure and we avoid tackling it.

Trap 9: No one knows about the benefits

Somewhere in a governance document there is a clear and simple articulation of the benefits and their links to business outcomes and strategic objectives. The document is shared among a few senior leaders and kept safely by the PMO. What a waste! This information would have created a powerful common goal to inform and inspire all those involved if only we'd have made it freely available. Instead we have confusion, conflict and inertia.

Trap 10: Did we do that?

One of the reasons it can be hard to find the right way to measure benefits is if our outcomes are so broad that they may be influenced by factors outside of our change. Take the example of a measure and target that reads '10 per cent increase in employee satisfaction scores'. This is likely to be influenced, positively or negatively, by a range of other factors outside of our control so we are unlikely to want to stake our career on achieving it. Alternatively, if the measure was narrowed to cover the responses to one or two questions in that survey which accurately reflect the scope of the change then that is easier to commit to.

Think...

1 Which of these traps is holding back your change?

2 Which one, if you fixed it, would bring the greatest benefit?

Profit ideas

Now you have identified some of the ways in which you are holding your organization back from effectively profiting from change what can you do to increase your chances of success?

Idea 1: Commit for the long haul

Benefits are the start and end of the change journey and as such require the most vigilance throughout the whole cycle. Structures and mechanisms to support their effective management must be available and in use from the very outset to the very end of the change cycle – longer than any other component. In fact both *directing* and *profiting* from change must be permanent embedded activities across the whole organization if they are to support effective change.

Idea 2: Get the ownership right

Your benefit owner needs to believe in the value of the benefits and therefore maintain their focus throughout the change. Engaging and maintaining the effective involvement of this person will be critical to keeping the change on track. If individual accountability is a natural part of the way you do business then you are probably already enjoying a sense of clarity and comfort knowing what you and others have to deliver. If clear accountability is not common then ensure your benefit owner is able to influence the decisions made throughout the change. Put in place appropriate support mechanisms to minimize the personal risk associated with the accountability of benefits ownership. Make sure you and your colleagues know who is accountable for setting, measuring, realigning and ultimately delivering the benefits needed.

Idea 3: Create and articulate the consequences of not delivering benefits

Ultimately if there are no consequences for not delivering benefits then why expend the energy to deliver them? Make it clear what will happen to the organization, its customers, divisions and the individual if benefits are not realized. One way of reinforcing these consequences is to align organization, department and individual performance targets to the change and business outcomes required. As with any measure, the trick is to make sure the measurement drives the right behaviour. Careful planning of KPIs, and an awareness of the behaviour they will drive and the ripple effects they will have makes them an influential lever for sustaining change if they are used wisely.

Idea 4: Make adjustments for your organization's culture

If your organization communicates openly and there is a high level of trust then your benefits are probably well founded. If, however, you hear phrases like 'they'll never sign off that much – leave out the...' 'we can't say the benefits are in jeopardy – take that out of the report' then there may be a significant gap between the reality of the costs and benefits and what appears in reports and is discussed in meetings. This undermines the whole process from the start so if you know the figures that are approved in your organization are usually 'sanitized' then you must realign expectations to the reality as soon as possible if the process is to have any credibility.

Idea 5: Embed the end-to-end benefits cycle into your organization

If you want to profit from all your hard work you will need to build a strong capability to reliably manage benefits throughout the change cycle; from identifying and articulating them at the outset, through constant monitoring, measurement and management throughout the change, to realizing and rewarding them at the end and reintegrating the achievements into the organization's roadmap of change. Provide benefit tracking tools, processes and systems that are appropriate to the type and nature of change in your organization. Make sure they are easy to use, accessible by the appropriate people and integrated into your current processes and frameworks. Consider a balanced scorecard approach to reporting shown in the example (Figure 4.6.8) below where the various interdependent aspects of a change are reported on simultaneously. For example, you could allocate a red amber or green status to each component of the cycle of change within your governance reporting with supplementary information about the reason for the status and the action being taken or decisions required to get the change back on track.

Idea 6: Work backwards from the organization's vision to your change

34 per cent of companies undertook projects that were not aligned with corporate strategy (Meskendahl et al, 2011).

There are two main reasons why your change should link to your organization's vision and strategy. Firstly, it provides a sense of meaning for those involved in and impacted by the change if they can see what it ultimately achieves and why it matters. Secondly, it will ensure scarce time, money and

Figure 4.6.8　Balanced scorecard

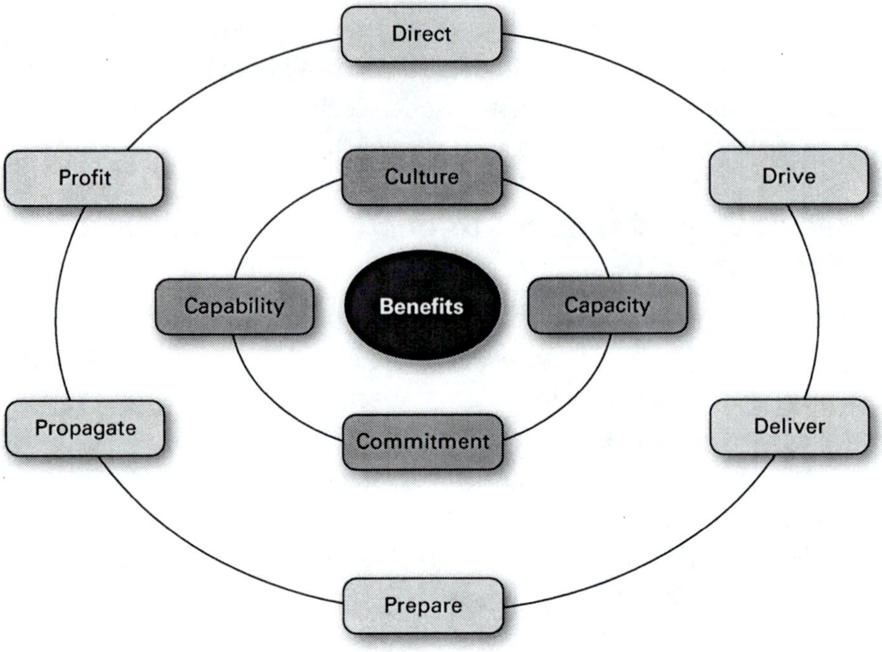

energy are focused on the valuable end result and is not tempted to work on things which don't help the organization make the progress it needs. Assuming your change will serve the strategy the best way to build the path is to start at the end! Figure 4.6.9 shows the questions to ask to pinpoint each step in the chain – from strategy through business and change outcomes to the change that is planned.

Idea 7: Prioritize benefits

Not all benefits are created equal and if you are going to be making trade-off decisions against the various benefits it will help to know which make a greater contribution than others. This prioritization should be done across the entire organization as something that appears to be less important for the delivery of one change may be a critical dependency for another.

Idea 8: Put your benefits in wet cement

A report from the UK government found that 'Benefits need to be actively managed – to ensure that forecast benefits are realized... and to capture

Figure 4.6.9 Understanding the path from strategy to change

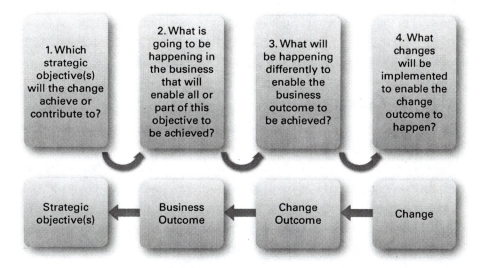

benefits that were not anticipated at the Business Case stage' (Jenner, 2007). Expect to update your benefits in response to new information. Some information will tell you your benefits are no longer sufficient or appropriate and some will provide opportunities to gain more value than originally planned. Symbolically this is important and logically it makes sense. Align your business and project governance to support this approach by validating and monitoring current benefits as well as being on the lookout for new, interim and better ones.

Idea 9: Get real

Most changes will be targeting some kind of financial benefit and it is wise to make sure you have set aside and continue to be aware of the real cost of the change. Governance processes can create a false sense of comfort by focusing only on the direct costs, for example project resources and IT costs. Attempts to stay within budget can mean that tasks are moved to areas where the cost is borne by another department and therefore becomes 'invisible'. As the chapter on *capacity* pointed out – the true cost of the change is much broader than direct project costs and it is that true cost that your organization is actually incurring. As you progress through the change additional costs will become evident and these may call into question the need for or scope of the change. For example, a project may outline in its business case that it will spend $1 million and deliver $2 million in benefits. If that organization does not adequately prepare its people for the changes the cost of the disruption to business performance through lost productivity, staff turnover and brand damage could be more than $1 million leaving them worse off than before and having wasted the investment.

Idea 10: Celebrate wins

Do this frequently and visibly whenever a change outcome, business outcome or benefit target is met. We all like to be rewarded and we will put effort into something which is clearly valued by our bosses. By celebrating the delivery of benefits your organization reinforces awareness of the whole change cycle and sends a strong message to its people that it is important. The celebration at the end should include a recap of why the change was started, the journey it has taken and the advantage the organization now has as a result. The clarity and commitment this portrays will add momentum to other changes in train and ensure greater commitment to future changes. This deliberate and visible activity makes your people feel their contribution, the obstacles they overcame and emotional rollercoaster they experienced ultimately delivered something worthwhile.

Think...

1   Which of these ideas could help your organization?

2   Which one would give you the most benefit?

So...

You started out on this change journey because you needed your organization to do, have or be something different but how will you know whether you've achieved what you now need? Appendix 11 contains a template to help you identify the specific change and business outcomes for your change as well as its link to your organizations strategy. The questions below will provide insights into how to improve your ability to realize those benefits.

1 What elements of our organization *support* the clear identification, reliable monitoring and successful realization of benefits? What can we do to strengthen the influence of these?

Culture_____

Processes_____

Policies_____

2 What elements of our organization *inhibit* the clear identification, reliable monitoring and successful realization of benefits? What can we do to reduce the influence of these?

Culture_____

Processes_____

Policies_____

3 Do we have a small number of benefits measures that are easy to monitor and agreed by those accountable?

_____

_____

_____

4 Do we monitor the relevance of our benefits and realign them in the light of new information?

_____

_____

_____

5 Are benefits used visibly to guide decision making during the delivery of the change?

_____

_____

_____

6 The most important thing I need to remember about *profiting* from change is ...

_____

_____

_____

Want to know more?

Search engine terms: value management, benefits management, benefits realization, value assessment, value measurement, return on investment.

What next?

Figure 5.0 **What next?**

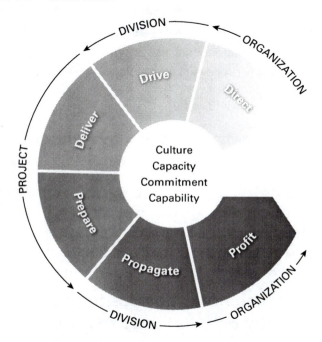

You will now have a better understanding of what it takes to change your organization reliably and sustainably. You will also have worked out how your organization stacks up – what you're good at and the gaps you may need to address.

Whilst the model is presented in a simple way to help you understand and analyse what is going on in your organization, the reality is that it is the **combination** of these attributes and activities that will dictate how successful your changes are. For example, if you have poor *delivery* you need to understand whether this is because you don't have the project management capability you need or is it actually a symptom of unclear *direction* or lack of *drive* from an active sponsor? Equally, if you identified a lack of focus on *preparing* for and *propagating* change, the successful *delivery* of a great solution can give a great sense of achievement but no benefits.

You are at the very beginning of a change – the change to improve the way your organization manages change. You will need a clear *direction*, to *drive* the improvements through, *deliver* and *prepare* your people for the changes, *propagate* them to make them stick and eventually *profit* from them in the form of improved organizational performance (faster, easier and more reliable business change). As with all changes, this one needs to fit within the change map for your organization and dovetail into other initiatives. Understanding the impacts and dependencies will be critical to developing a clear direction. By using current business improvements to develop and trial new change capability, processes and systems you will be able to get immediate feedback.

Step 1: Work out whether you have enough of what it takes

Does the organization have what it takes to improve change capability? Look at your answers to the questions and assessments in the 'C' chapters and appendices – culture, capacity, commitment and capability – and assess your organization's readiness to embark on the improvements.

Step 2: Perform an honest assessment of how well you currently do what needs to be done

As you have worked through the book you will have had the opportunity to identify the strengths and weaknesses in the way you manage change. Think about what this means for your planned improvements. If you know there is little clear direction or that people are typically unprepared for changes, how will this impact on your success? What can you do to mitigate those risks? Summarize your strengths and weaknesses and understand the implications. Using your new knowledge from throughout the book, pull together a summary of where you think your organization is performing well and where it needs to improve. Use the template in Appendix 12 to help you.

Step 3: Set the direction for your change

Clearly articulate what needs to change, why the improvements need to happen, why now and how they support the organization's strategy. Articulate a clear vision of what success will look like. To develop your prioritized list of improvements think about the following.

Maintain your strengths

Think carefully about what has led you to be competent in these areas and how sustainable this competence is. Can it be sustained without further monitoring and intervention? Are the systems, processes and capability that support this performance embedded in your organization or dependent on a few key individuals who could move on at any time?

Address your weaknesses

It is always easier not to change so think about the consequences of not improving these areas. Depending on your organization and the type of changes you need to roll out, you may find that some of the weak areas can stay weak with very little impact. You will also find that the right improvements to one or two of the more important elements will deliver a significant uplift in your performance.

Decide which to tackle first

Understanding your starting point and the type of change your organization will go through will inform your approach. Now that you understand where some of the traps may be and which ideas you need to install or extend, think carefully about which order to tackle them in. Depending on the level of influence you have, some changes can be implemented more quickly or easily than others. If you scored low on the Cs (*culture, capacity, commitment* and *capability*) these will have the greatest impact on your ability to change and are also among the hardest and time consuming to fix. Improving areas like *direction* and *profit* need changes which cross the whole organization. Improvements to the way you deliver and prepare for change requires realignment of your processes, systems and capabilities in project teams.

Step 4: Find the right driver

Identify the person (is it you?) with enough power and interest to be the driving force behind the improvements.

Step 5: Deliver the change

Work with all those involved to agree priorities, allocate resources and design, build and test the best solutions. Report regularly on progress against interim goals and planned benefits using the Cycle of Change model as a reporting framework. Draw on the balanced scorecard approach from the last chapter and use a format similar to that shown in Figure 5.1 to provide additional information to governance forums.

Step 6: Prepare everyone and everything

Improving the way you plan and manage change will inevitably mean that people and other elements of today's business will need to change what they do, how they do it and the tools and processes they use. Make as many as possible of the changes you'll need before introducing the improvements.

Step 7: Propagate the improvements

Give the changes the time and attention required after implementation to make sure they stick and are delivering real value. Expect to refine them once people start using them.

Step 8: Profit from the improvements

Celebrate the achievements that increased change capability is bringing to the organization.

Finally... get the most out of the information in this book. Remember you can use it to educate, assess current performance, manage risk, develop and test methodologies frameworks and governance processes and forums. Keep it around you for reference. If you get a hunch or some data that tells you your change is not going well, have another look at the model and think about which area may be causing the problem. Do you not have enough of one of the Cs or are you not putting the required effort into the Ds or the Ps?

Figure 5.1 Cycle of change status report

Cycle of change component	Green/ Amber/ Red Status	Explanation	Consequences	Action	Owner
Do we have sufficient and appropriate...					
Culture					
Capacity					
Commitment					
Capability					
Do We...					
Direct					
Drive					
Deliver					
Prepare					
Propagate					
Profit					

Appendix 1

Cycle of Change Model mapped to Kotter's eight steps[29]

Whilst John Kotter himself has since expanded on his original model aimed at change leaders, it is still frequently referred to within organizations. Therefore, it might be useful to have this handy cross reference to show how the Cycle of Change Model covers and provides a deeper understanding of the elements in Kotter's famous eight steps.

Table: Appendix 1

Kotter's Eight Steps of Organizational Change	Cycle of Change Model
Urgency	DIRECT (and DRIVE)
Coalition	DRIVE (and COMMITMENT)
Vision	DIRECT
Communicate vision	DRIVE (and COMMITMENT)
Remove obstacles	DRIVE, DELIVER and PREPARE
Short-term wins	DELIVER
Build on the change	PROPAGATE (and CAPABILITY)
Anchor the change	PROPAGATE and PROFIT (and CAPABILITY)

Appendix 2

Cultural assessment

This tool will help you articulate the cultural forces that will either help or hinder your change. Start by taking a look at the statements below and use the 'Response' column to uncover the reality in your organization. Then move on to the 'Potential impact' column and think through what this means for your change – in what way might it help or get in the way? Mark an 'X' in the column you think describes the force of the impact on your change. Will it help or hinder? A little or a lot? When you have finished, allocate the weightings shown at the end of the assessment and calculate your final score to find out if your change can succeed.

Table: Appendix 2

	Statement	Response(s)	Potential impact on your change	Hinder a lot	Hinder a little	No effect	Help a little	Help a lot
Example	I am/am not held accountable for the things I say I'll do	*It's really clear who is accountable for what. I am regularly asked for progress reports on the areas I am responsible for.*	*This will be useful when we need leaders to take responsibility for embedding the change and motivating their team.*					X
External	1. The people delivering, leading and receiving the change are all from the same national or other external cultural background							
Accountability	2. I am/am not held accountable for the things I say I'll do							

Table: Appendix 2 Continued

	Statement	Response(s)	Potential impact on your change	Hinder a lot	Hinder a little	No effect	Help a little	Help a lot
Communication	3. My organization mostly communicates... two-way or one-way; frequently or infrequently; to the point or verbose; in plain language or using jargon; using a conversational style or a more formal tone; from and to all levels and areas of the organization or only a few levels or areas?							
Customs	4. New people are often frustrated by the way we...							
	5. I like coming to work because our organization...							
	6. People usually leave our organization because...							
Decision making	7. Getting decisions made is (quick/slow easy/hard)...							

Table: Appendix 2   Continued

	Statement	Response(s)	Potential impact on your change	Hinder a lot	Hinder a little	No effect	Help a little	Help a lot
Leaders	8. Our leaders take calculated risks	True/False						
	9. Suggestions from all levels of the organization are taken seriously and actively considered	True/False						
	10. Our leadership team work for the good of the organization even if it is to the detriment of their business unit	True/False						
	11. Change is talked about in a positive way and is seen as an opportunity	True/False						
Making mistakes	12. When we have a problem it is reported quickly and the priority is on fixing and learning from it.	True/False						

Table: Appendix 2 Continued

	Statement	Response(s)	Potential impact on your change	Hinder a lot	Hinder a little	No effect	Help a little	Help a lot
Rewards	13. The successful people in our organization are those that...							
	14. I am/My team is generally a. rewarded for ... b. and penalized for...							
Priorities	15. When money is tight we a. cut... b. and spend on...							
	16. When time is tight we make sure we still a. do... b. and we do less of or stop...							
	17. I/We respond a. quickly to... b. and slowly to...							
View of organization	18. When my team can talk freely they say about the organization...							

Table: Appendix 2 Continued

Statement	Response(s)	Potential impact on your change	Hinder a lot	Hinder a little	No effect	Help a little	Help a lot
		Step 1 Add up the number of 'X' in each column			0		
		Step 2 Multiply that total by the weighting indicated	X –10 = –	X –5 = –	0	X 5 = +	X10 = +
		Step 3 Add the numbers together					

Example:

			Hinder a lot	Hinder a little	No effect	Help a little	Help a lot
		Step 1 Add up the number of 'X' in each column	3	7	2	3	3
		Step 2 Multiply that number by the appropriate amount	X –10 = –30	X –5 = –35	0	X 5 = +15	X10 = +30
		Step 3 Add the numbers together			–20		

Use the total score to assess your overall chances of success. Have you got more working for you than against you? If the 'helping' factors are strong enough and can be exploited, you can often use these to overcome the negative forces.

Figure Appendix 2.1   Negative total

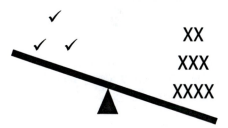

If the total number is negative you have more working against you than for you and you can expect the change to feel like an uphill struggle. The larger the number, the more difficult it will be.

Figure Appendix 2.2   Positive total

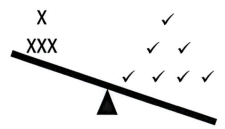

If the total number is positive you have more working in your favour than against it and you can expect your change to feel like a relatively smooth process. The larger the number, the easier it will be.

Figure Appendix 2.3   Zero total

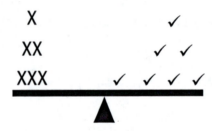

If the total number is zero you have equal forces at play. These forces will be working hard to maintain the status quo so you should not be complacent.

Next steps: Use the information in the 'Potential Impact' column to help you plan your approach. Add activities to your strategy and plan which will exploit the positive forces and mitigate or work around the negative ones.

Appendix 3

Capacity assessment

This tool will help you articulate the capacity you need and the strategy to make it. Assuming you are embarking on your change start in the left-hand column by listing the time people equipment and money you'll need to design and build the change. In the next column write down the strategy that you are using or will use to access what you need. Move to the box at the bottom of the page and identify any major gaps or risks that this analysis has identified and what you need to do to address them. The content of this box can provide useful information for change governance forums and decisions. Repeat the process for the transition and post-implementation periods.

Table: Appendix 3

	Designing and building the change		Transitioning to the new way		Period after the change has been introduced	
	Capacity required	Strategy for making available	Capacity required	Strategy for making available	Capacity required	Strategy for making available
Time						
People (1)						
Equipment						
Money						
Major gaps and risks						

(1) Change deliverers, receivers and leaders

Appendix 4

Commitment assessment

This tool will help you articulate the groups involved in and impacted by the change. It will also help you plan the activities required to create and maintain the level of commitment you'll need from each group. Start in the left-hand column by identifying the various groups involved in delivering, leading and receiving the change. Answer the questions in the subsequent columns to identify their current and required level of commitment and the activities you'll need.

Table: Appendix 4

Stakeholder Group	What do they need to commit to?		What level of commitment is required?		What will we do to build the commitment we need?	
	Require commitment to…	Currently committed to…	Level of commitment required	Actual level of commitment	Strategy to build commitment	Strategy to maintain commitment
Change Deliverers 1. 2. 3.						
Change Leaders 1. 2. 3.						
Change Receivers 1. 2. 3.						

Appendix 5

Capability assessment

This tool will help you plan how to access the capability you need to change successfully (see Figure 3.4.2 for an example). Start by identifying the non-technical and technical capability that you already have and what you'll need in the future. In the next columns estimate how long you'll need that capability for and whether it is core or non-core to your business. For each capability decide if you will transition it out, maintain it or, if it is new, whether you will buy or build it. Finally outline the plan you need to put in place to provide the capability your organization will need.

Table: Appendix 5

Have	Need	Dur'n	Core (in-house)	Non-core (buy/hire)	Transition out	Maintain	Build/buy	Plan
Non-technical capability								
Technical capability								

Appendix 6

Elevator pitch

This tool will help you develop the standard way of talking about the change. Complete the following statements **using no more than two sentences for each**. Make sure everyone agrees to it and use it constantly and consistently to talk about the change.

Table: Appendix 6

The vision for our organization is ...	
... and the strategic objective that our change helps to deliver is ...	
... so the business outcomes we must achieve are...	*(Outcomes and benefits)*
We are changing because ...	*(Why?)*
We are changing now because ...	*(Why now?)*
We are changing ...	*(What?)*
The people who will be impacted are ...	*(Who and how?)*

Appendix 7

Driver checklist

This tool will help you to identify and brief a suitable change driver, identify gaps in their skills or activities and plans to address these. Tick the boxes that apply to your change driver then use the next column to identify any gaps in their activities, characteristics or attributes. In the next column work out what risk this represents to the success of your change and in the final column the strategies you will use to mitigate those risks.

Table: Appendix 7

	Gap	Risk to success of change	Strategy to mitigate risk
Our change driver …	☐ Safeguards the change on behalf of the organization ☐ Is an advocate for the change ☐ Brings the *direction* to life ☐ Maintains an appropriate level of energy throughout the change ☐ Balances project activity with business priorities ☐ Maintains a healthy and productive working environment ☐ Removes obstacles ☐ Communicates effectively to a wide range of people through a wide range of channels ☐ Enlists and maintain the support of others		
Our change driver has…	☐ A genuine belief in the value of the change ☐ Skin in the game ☐ Authority ☐ Business focus ☐ A stable future ☐ Capacity to perform the role ☐ Experience		

Table: Appendix 7 Continued

		Gap	Risk to success of change	Strategy to mitigate risk
Our change driver is …	☐ A good role model ☐ Influential ☐ A good communicator ☐ A principled negotiator ☐ Seen as a fair leader ☐ Able to empower people ☐ Open to new information ☐ A strategic thinker ☐ Realistic			
Our change driver demonstrates…	☐ Self-awareness ☐ High emotional intelligence ☐ A high tolerance for ambiguity and risk ☐ A low need for control ☐ Persistence ☐ Resilience			

Appendix 8

Delivery governance maturity assessment

This tool will help you identify your organization's current and required delivery governance maturity and how to build the additional maturity required. Start by marking the element on each line that best represents the level of maturity you need to govern the scale, rate and complexity of future change in your organization. Then using a different colour mark the level of maturity you believe your organization is at currently. Finally complete the strategy column on the right by jotting down some ideas for how you can fill the gap.

Table: Appendix 8
Delivery Governance Maturity Level Indicators

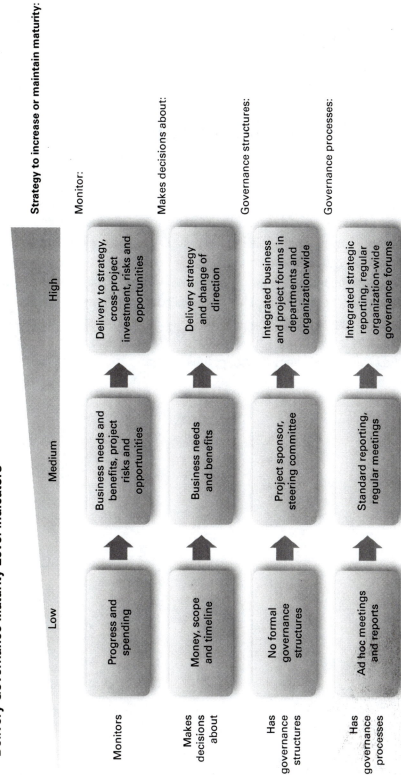

Strategy to increase or maintain maturity:

	Low	Medium	High	
Monitors	Progress and spending	Business needs and benefits, project risks and opportunities	Delivery to strategy, cross-project investment, risks and opportunities	Monitor:
Makes decisions about	Money, scope and timeline	Business needs and benefits	Delivery strategy and change of direction	Makes decisions about:
Has governance structures	No formal governance structures	Project sponsor, steering committee	Integrated business and project forums in departments and organization-wide	Governance structures:
Has governance processes	Ad hoc meetings and reports	Standard reporting, regular meetings	Integrated strategic reporting, regular organization-wide governance forums	Governance processes:

Appendix 9

Impact assessment and change strategy

This tool will enable you to record the people impacted, the nature of that impact and what you need to do to make them and their environment ready for the change. Start by listing the groups you know will be impacted in the first column then for each one decide how disruptive the change is likely to be for them and record the way in which they will be impacted. In the next column record anything that will either help or hinder your change – for example the culture, current practices or artefacts. Finally, jot down some ideas in the final columns for the things you will need to do or provide to make the people and the environment ready to accept the change.

Table: Appendix 9

Stakeholder Group (Internal and External)	Impact of the change		Environmental factors to consider		Change approach and activities	
	High/ Med/ Low	Description of impact	Will support the change	Will undermine the change	People readiness	Environmental readiness

Appendix 10

Planning to make change stick

This tool will help to plan how you will measure whether your change is being adopted, embedded and sustained sufficiently and appropriately to enable benefits to be delivered. Work with the project team and the people impacted to agree the best measures and targets. Work from the left clearly articulating the data you will collect and who will collect it. Then complete the flow of this information by providing details of the reporting and the decision making associated with each measure. Finally, acknowledge the risks associated with each measure, the target or reporting. In particular think about how human nature will impact on the effectiveness of these measures.

Table: Appendix 10

The evidence we will use to tell us whether the change has stuck is... (measure)	The target we are aiming for is... (target)	Therefore the data we need to collect is... (data – what, how, when)	Who will collect it?	When will it be reported? (To whom, how often)	Accountable decision maker	Risks and mitigation plans

Appendix 11

Planning to profit from the change

This tool will help you identify the steps from the delivery of your change through to a more successful organization. In the first row answer the questions 1 to 4 on page 275. Then for each one work out how you will measure whether you have achieved it, what target you need to set and any interim indicators that you'll need to make sure you remain on track. Putting this together should be a collaborative exercise and the resulting coherent story should form the basis of all communication.

Table: Appendix 11

1. Which strategic objective(s) will the change achieve or contribute to?

2. What is going to be happening in the business that will enable all or part of this objective to be achieved?

3. What will be happening differently to enable the business outcome to be achieved?

4. What changes will be implemented to enable the change outcome to happen?

Strategic objective(s) → Business Outcome → Change Outcome → Change

The strategic objective(s) this change will contribute to is …	The contribution it will make is …	The outcome the change will enable is …	The change we will make is …
Measure:	Measure:	Measure:	Measure:
Target:	Target:	Target:	Target:
Interim Indicators:	Interim Indicators:	Interim Indicators:	Interim Indicators:

Appendix 12

Action planning

Use this tool to summarize the insights you have had about how your organization manages change and start to plan the improvements. Start by summarizing the strengths and weaknesses in each area and rate your organization out of 10 for each component. Decide the relative importance of each and jot down some high-level strategies you could use to improve each area and the risks you are likely to encounter. Next return to Chapter 5 and follow the steps – starting setting the direction.

Table: Appendix 12

	Strengths we need to maintain	Weaknesses or gaps we may need to address	Mark out of 10	Priority H/M/L	Implications	Strategy	Risks and mitigation plans
The four things we need to have…							
Culture to support change							
Capacity to think about and make change happen							
Commitment to the right things to enable change to happen							
Capability in all areas needed to make the change happen							
		Total C's					

Table: Appendix 12   Continued

	Strengths we need to maintain	Weaknesses or gaps we may need to address	Mark out of 10	Priority H/M/L	Implications	Strategy	Risks and mitigation plans
The six things we need to do well …							
Direct the change							
Drive the change							
Deliver the change							
Prepare for the change							
Propagate the change							
Profit from the change							
		Total D's & P's					
		Add the score for C's to the score for D's and P's to give you your total score out of one hundred					

Notes

1   IBM, 2010. IBM Capitalising on Complexity May 2010
    http://www-935.ibm.com/services/au/ceo/ceostudy2010/gbe03297usen.pdf

2   Lewin, 1951.

3   Eaton, 2010; in 1995 Kotter said only 30% succeeded; Miller (2002) reported
    that 70% of change programmes fail; Higgs and Rowland (2005) said 'only
    one in four or five change programmes actually succeed'; the Standish
    Group report (2009) shows more project failing and less successful projects;
    Maurer, 2010.

4   Webb, 2010.

5   Yatco, 1999; Locke and Schweiger, 1979.

6   HBR Ideacast, 2010. Interview with Shawn Achor.

7   Karla Brandau, Business Tips: Brain Engagement and Discretionary Effort
    http://www.mindconnection.com/library/business/brainengagement.htm

8   Dwyer, 2011.

9   Kahneman, Knetsch and Thaler, 1990.

10 Amabile and Kramer, 2010.

11 http://www.brainyquote.com/quotes/quotes/e/erichoffer109153.html

12 http://www.goodreads.com/quotes/185636-if-the-rate-of-change-on-the-out-
    side-exceeds-the

13 HBR IdeaCast, 2011a. Interview with Paul Nunes.

14 HBR IdeaCast, 2011b. Interview with John Donahoe.

15 http://www.goodreads.com/author/quotes/79014.Yogi_Berra

16 Lovallo and Mendonca, 2007.

17 Favaro, Karlsson and Neilson, 2011; Kirdahy, 2008; Dandira, 2011.

18 Hansens, Ibarra and Peyer, 2013.

19 Sparks, 2002.

20 Lovallo and Sibony, 2010.

21 Prosci change management webinar: Top trends in change management.
    http://www.change-management.com/Prosci-Top-Trends-Webinar-Slides.pdf

22 Change Management Institute, 2012.

23   Australian Institute of Project Management Survey March 2011. http://www.
      aipm.com.au/AIPM/3G/P/poll_results.aspx?WebsiteKey=189213da-560d-4cef-
      8ae9-fc492d9a261b 'Is change management a subset of project. manage-
      ment? Yes: 541 votes, 72%; No: 154 votes, 21%; They are the same: 40 votes,
      5%; Don't know: 12 votes, 2%.'

24   Lawson and Price, 2003. See reference to David Kolb.

25   Examples include Campbell and Pritchard, 1976; Kanfer, 1990;
      Latham and Pinder, 2005; Mitchell and Daniels, 2003; Vroom, 1964.
      Cited in Pritchard et al, 2008.

26   Schneider, Brief and Guzzo, 1996.

27   Quoted in Mansour and Gomolski, 2006.

28   Lingle and Schiemann, 1996.

29   Kotter, 1996.

References

Achor, S (2011) *The Happiness Advantage*, Virgin Books, London

Amabile, Theresa and Kramer, Steven J (2010) The HBR List: Breakthrough Ideas for 2010, 1: What Really Motivates Workers, *Harvard Business Review*, The Magazine (January), http://hbr.org/2010/01/the-hbr-list-breakthrough-ideas-for-2010/ar/

Amabile, Theresa and Kramer, Steven J (2012) How leaders kill meaning at work, *The McKinsey Quarterly*, (1), pp 124–31

Anderson, Nick and Nwosu, Kelly (2012) Focusing change to win: global survey findings of business leaders and consultants, New Catalyst, Washington DC, http://www.academia.edu/1597979/Focusing_Change_to_Win

Bahrami, H (1992) The emerging flexible organization: Perspectives from Silicon Valley, *California Management Review*, **34** (4), pp 33–52

Booz Allen Hamilton (2002) Building a methodology for measuring the value of e-services, Booz Allen & Hamilton and Harvard Kennedy School of Government, US Social Security Administration, US General Services Administration

Brandau, Karla (nd) Business Tips: Brain Engagement and Discretionary Effort, Mindconnection, http://www.mindconnection.com/library/business/brainengagement.htm

Campbell, J P and Pritchard, R D (1976) Motivation theory in industrial and organizational psychology, in *Handbook of Industrial and Organzational Psychology*, ed M D Dunnette, pp 63–130, Rand McNally, Chicago

Change Management Institute (2012) Change Management Practitioner Competencies, https://www.change-management-institute.com/sites/default/files/CMI_CMPractitionerCompetencyModel_2012%20V2.2.pdf

Change Management Institute (2012) Organisational Change Management Maturity Model, https://www.change-management-institute.com/sites/default/files/CMI%20White%20Paper,%20Change%20Agility%20-%20Feb%202012.pdf

Claver, E, Llopis, J, Garcia, D and Molina, H (1998) Organizational culture for innovation and new technological behavior, *Journal of High Technology Management Research*, B (1), pp 55–68

Dandira, Martin (2011) The impact of executive directors' service contracts on strategic plan, *Business Strategy Series*, **12** (1), pp 12–18

Denison, D R and Mishra, A K (1995) Toward a theory of organizational culture and effectiveness, *Organization Science*, **6** (2) (March–April), pp 204–23

Dwyer, K (2011) Engagement Trends Q4 2010, Change Factory, Melbourne, http://www.changefactory.com.au

Eaton, Mark (2010) Why change programs fail, *Training Journal*, (February), pp 53–57

Ericsson, Anders K, Prietula, Michael J and Cokely, Edward T (2007) The making of an expert, *Harvard Business Review* (July–August), http://hbr.org/2007/07/the-making-of-an-expert

Faull, N and Fleming, P (2005) Turning intentions into outcomes: a quick scorecard to guide implementation, *Measuring Business Excellence*, **9** (3), p 7

Favaro, K, Karlsson, P and Neilson, G L (2011) CEO Succession 2010: the four types of CEOs, Strategy & business, Booz & Co (Summer) (63), p 10, http://www.booz.com/media/file/BoozCo-CEO-Succession-2010-Four-Types.pdf

Hansens, Morten T, Ibarra, Herminia and Peyer, Urs (2013) 100 Best performing CEO's in the world, *Harvard Business Review*, (Jan–Feb), p 81

HBR IdeaCast (2010) Why a happy brain performs better: interview with Shawn Achor, HBR Blog Network, 25 November 2010, http://blogs.hbr.org/2010/11/why-a-happy-brain-performs-bet/

HBR IdeaCast (2011a) The Holy Grail of continuous growth, interview with Paul Nunes, HBR Blog Network, 13 January, http://blogs.hbr.org/2011/01/the-holy-grail-of-continuous-g/

HBR IdeaCast (2011b) eBay's CEO on Growth, Acquisitions, and Going Mobile: interview with John Donahoe, HBR Blog Network, 21 January, http://blogs.hbr.org/2011/01/ebays-ceo-on-growth-acquisitio/

Heath, C and Heath, D (2010) *Switch: How to change things when change is hard*, Random House, London

Henry, David with Jespersen, Frederick F (2002) Mergers: why most big deals don't pay off, *Business Week*, 14 October

Higgs, M and Rowland, D (2005) All changes great and small: exploring approaches to change and its leadership, *Journal of Change Management*, **5** (2), pp 121–51

Human Capital Magazine (2010) 12 September, pp 12–19 http://www.hcamag.com/

IBM (2010) *Capitalising on Complexity: Insights from the global chief executive officer study*, IBM Global Business Services, Somers, NY

Jenner, Stephen (2007) Managing the Portfolio, Realising the Benefits, Office for Criminal Justice Reform UK (CJS), http://www.epractice.eu/files/documents/cases/253-1181234565.pdf

Kahneman, D, Knetsch, J L and Thaler, R H (1990) Experimental tests of the endowment effect and the Coase Theorem, *Journal of Political Economy*, **98** (6) pp 1325–48

Kanfer, R (1990) Motivation theory and industrial and organizational psychology, in *Handbook of Industrial and Organzational Psychology*, ed M D Dunnette, 2 edn, pp 75–130, Consulting Psychologists Press, Palo Alto, CA

Kelman, Herbert (1958) Compliance, identification and internalization: three processes of attitude change, *The Journal of Conflict Resolution*, **2** (1), pp 51–60

Kirdahy, Matthew (2008) CEO Turnover Increased In 2007, Forbes.com, 7 March, http://www.forbes.com/2008/03/07/executive-ceo-tenure-lead-manage-cx_mk_0307turnover.html

Kotter, John P (1996) *Leading Change*, Harvard Business School Press, Boston, MA

Kotter, John P (2008) *A Sense of Urgency*, Harvard Business Publishing, Watertown, MA

KPMG (2005) Global IT project management survey: how committed are you?, KPMG International, Switzerland, http://www.totalmetrics.com/function-points-downloads/IT-Project-Governance.pdf

Latham, G P and Pinder, C C (2005) Work motivation theory and research at the dawn of the twenty-first century, *Annual Review of Psychology*, 56, pp 495–516

Lawson, Emily and Price, Colin (2003) The psychology of change management, *The McKinsey Quarterly*, Special Edition: Organization (June)

Lewin, K (ed) (1951) *Field Theory in Social Science: Selected theoretical papers*, Harper & Row, New York

Lingle, J H and Schiemann, W A (1996) From balanced scorecard to strategic gauges: is measurement worth it?, *Management Review*, **85** (3), pp 56–61

LIW (2009) Organisational Leadership Architecture: Why organisations need leadership more than leaders. Leading Initiatives Worldwide, Mosman NSW, Australia

Locke, E A and Schweiger, D M (1979) Participation in decision-making: one more look, *Research in Organisational Behaviour*, 1, pp 265–339

Lovallo, Dan P and Mendonca, Lenny T (2007) Strategy's strategist: an interview with Richard Rumelt, *The McKinsey Quarterly*, (4), pp 56–67

Lovallo, Dan and Sibony, Oliver (2010) The case for behavioral strategy, *The McKinsey Quarterly*, (2), pp 30–45

Mansour, George A and Gomolski, Barbara (2006) How to optimize IT investment decisions: are you maximizing business value or merely 'satisficing'?, Gartner Research (July) http://www.gartner.com/id=494223

Maurer, Rick (2010) *Beyond the Wall of Resistance: Why 70% of changes still fail and what you can do about it*, 2nd edn, Bard Press, Austin, TX

McKinsey Quarterly (2006) The McKinsey global survey of business executives: business and society, *The McKinsey Quarterly*, (2), pp 33–39 https://www.mckinseyquarterly.com/PDFDownload.aspx?ar=1809

Meskendahl, Sascha, Jonas, Daniel, Kock, Alexander and Gemünden Hans Georg (2011) The art of project portfolio management, multiprojectmanagement.org (July), https://www.tim.tu-berlin.de/fileadmin/fg101/TIM_Working_Paper_Series/Volume_4/MPM-Artikel.pdf

Miller, D (2002) Successful change leaders: what makes them? What do they do that is different?, *Journal of Change Management*, **2** (4), pp 359–68

Mitchell, T R and Daniels, D (2003) Motivation, in *Handbook of Psychology, vol 12: Industrial/organizational psychology*, eds W Borman, D Ilgen and P Klimoski, pp 225–54, Wiley, New York

Nunes, P and Breene, T (2011) Reinvent your business before it's too late, *Harvard Business Review*, The Magazine, (January)

Parry, W and Kirsch, C (2011) Taking the guesswork out of change management, presentation, Change Management Institute Conference, Sydney

Pritchard, Robert D, Harrell, Melissa M, DiazGranados, Deborah and Guzman, Melissa J (2008) The productivity measurement and enhancement system: a meta-analysis, *Journal of Applied Psychology*, **93** (3), pp 540–67

Rock, David (2009) *Your Brain at Work: Strategies for overcoming distraction, regaining focus, and working smarter all day long*, Harper Business, New York

Roxburgh, Charles (2003) Hidden flaws in strategy, *The McKinsey Quarterly*, (2), http://www.mckinsey.com/insights/strategy/hidden_flaws_in_strategy

Schneider, Benjamin, Brief, Arthur P and Guzzo, Richard A (1996) Creating a climate and culture for sustainable organizational change, *Organizational Dynamics*, **24** (4), pp 6–19

Senge, Peter M (1990) *The Fifth Discipline*, Random House, London

Senge, P (1999) Generating profound change, in *The Dance of Change: The challenge of sustaining momentum in learning organisations*, ed P Senge, C Roberts, R Ross, B Smith George Roth and A Kleiner, Nicholas Brealey, London

Smith, M (1998) The development of an innovation culture, *Management Accounting*, **76** (2), pp 22–24

Sparks, Dennis (2002) Inner conflicts, inner strengths: an interview with Robert Kegan and Lisa Lahey, *Journal of Staff Development* (Summer) **23** (3), pp 66–71

Standish Group (2009) *CHAOS Summary 2009* (April), Boston, MA

Tranzform Group (2009) Benefits realisation poll: is your organisation really setting up its projects to guarantee achievement of the expected benefits?, Sydney, Australia

Tucker, Chuck (2004) Building brilliant business cases, Gartner Executive Programs, 1 January, http://www.gartner.com/id=421294

Vroom, V H (1964) *Work and Motivation*, Wiley, New York

Webb, Allen (2010) Making the emotional case for change: an interview with Chip Heath, *The McKinsey Quarterly*, (2), http://www.mckinsey.com/insights/organization/making_the_emotional_case_for_change_an_interview_with_chip_heath

Yatco, Mei C (1999) Joint Application Design/Development, System Analysis, Management Information Systems (MIS) Program, School of Business Administration, University of Missouri-St Louis, http://www.umsl.edu/~sauterv/analysis/JAD.html

Index

NB: page numbers in *italics* indicate figures or tables

Also available from **Kogan Page**

Find out more; visit **www.koganpage.com** and
sign up for offers and regular e-newsletters.

CPSIA information can be obtained at www.ICGtesting.com
Printed in the USA
BVOW04s0036020514
352372BV00002B/4/P